A DICTIONARY AND GLOSSARY
FOR THE IRISH LITERARY REVIVAL

BY THE SAME AUTHOR

An Anglo-Irish Dialect Glossary for Joyce's Works

A
Dictionary and Glossary
for the
Irish Literary Revival

Richard Wall

First published in 1995 by Colin Smythe Limited,
Gerrards Cross, Buckinghamshire

British Library Cataloguing in Publication Data

A record of this book is available
from the British Library

ISBN 0-86140-359-2

Printed in Great Britain
by T. J. Press (Padstow) Ltd., Cornwall

For Clair, Deirdre, Siobhan,
Aisling and Ciara

CONTENTS

7

PREFACE

"All the time he kept on treasuring with condign
satisfaction each and every crumb of trektalk,
covetous of his neighbour's word . . . ."
(Joyce, *Finnegans Wake*, 172.29-30)

This work has its genesis in *An Anglo-Irish Dialect Glossary for Joyce's Works* (Colin Smythe, 1986; Syracuse University Press, 1987). Indeed, as soon as I began that project, I realized that my fascination with the English language in Irish literature would eventually lead me to produce this work.

I first became vaguely aware of my subject while growing up in Dublin. Occasionally, I wondered why I never heard on the BBC "Home Service," or saw in the English boys' books I read, many of the words and phrases my friends and I used regularly, and that they used words and phrases we never used. While English boys played truant, we went *miching*. They spoke disparagingly of cads and bounders; we spoke of *sleveens* and *gobshites*. When I moved to Canada, I became much more conscious of my subject, when I discovered, somewhat to my surprise, that many words and phrases I used, and assumed were standard English, were not. My academic interest in the subject began when I attended the late Professor Alan Bliss's seminars on the Anglo-Irish dialect at University College, Dublin (At that time, Professor Bliss was, on behalf of the Royal Irish Academy Committee for the Study of Anglo-Irish Language and Literature, attempting to get a projected *Anglo-Irish Dictionary* under way). While writing my doctoral dissertation on James Joyce's theories of art and the artist, I happened to discover that his massive use of Hiberno-English (he called it Anglo-Irish), particularly in works such as *Ulysses* and *Finnegans Wake*, frequently caused his commentators serious problems; and it was this discovery that first tempted me to write on the subject of this work.

I am indebted to a number of individuals and institutions for

9

assistance and encouragement in the preparation of this work: the late Professor Alan Bliss of University College Dublin, for his encouragement, advice and perceptive comments on my early efforts; my colleague and friend, Professor James Black, a native of Ballymena, Co. Antrim, for not taking a *scunner* against me for my interminable questions about Ulster-English; my many colleagues and friends in the International Association for the Study of Anglo-Irish Literature for their interest and encouragement; The University of Calgary for financial assistance and allowing me the invaluable opportunity of spending a sabbatical leave in Dublin; the staff of The University of Calgary Library, the National Library of Ireland and the Library of Trinity College Dublin; the Royal Irish Academy for allowing me to consult its Anglo-Irish Word Lists; and, finally, my wife Clair, who proof-read and commented on this work, and who, consciously and unconsciously, contributed much to its content.

Publication of this work has been made possible in part by a grant from the Endowment Fund of The University of Calgary.

Richard Wall

University of Calgary

INTRODUCTION

This work is intended to provide the general reader, as well as the specialist, with a guide to a major aspect of the language of Irish literature in English during the period of the Irish Literary Revival. The existence and interaction in Ireland of two linguistic and cultural traditions, Irish and English, over a very long period of history, and a third tradition which has its genesis in the seventeenth-century Plantation of Ulster, make the task of finding terms and providing definitions that are precise and universally acceptable virtually impossible. The earliest term used for the results of this interaction, Anglo-Irish, was first used about the end of the eighteenth century to describe the English settlers or their descendants in Ireland and, in time, their literature and language.[1] The term has obvious historical, political, social, and even religious connotations, and is questionable on logical grounds; nevertheless, it is now the most widely used term for literature written in English by Irish writers, and, until recently, for the variety or varieties of English used in Ireland. What to call this literature and language, and even the meaning of the various terms used, is a perennial subject of debate among scholars. The debate is, ultimately, not a literary or linguistic issue; it is socio-political. This is hardly surprising. In matters relating to Ireland, an island with a turbulent history, that is now partitioned, with each part having a variety of official and unofficial names, and each name conveying its own burden of emotive baggage, the act of naming invariably has complex socio-political implications. In this work, I simply follow the current convention of calling the literature Anglo-Irish and the language Hiberno-English.

Determining the limits of Hiberno-English is as difficult a task as defining it. Since it is a contact vernacular, largely the product of the interaction of cultures and languages over a long period of history, it does not have precise limits. There is a large grey area between Hiberno-English and Irish (Gaelic) on the one hand, and

---

[1] The date of the earliest use of the term recorded in the *Oxford English Dictionary* is 1792.

11

standard English on the other. Since the primary purpose of this work is to elucidate literature, it errs on the side of inclusiveness in its treatment of marginal terms. *Aisling*, for example, is an Irish word and its definition is available in any dictionary of Irish, and *smugging* is an English dialect word accessible in the *English Dialect Dictionary*. Both are included because they are part of the currency of Hiberno-English and not defined in dictionaries of standard English. The former, which is a term of particular significance in Irish and Anglo-Irish literature (and now a popular name for girls), is found in Joyce's *Finnegans Wake* and Seamus Heaney's "An Open Letter"; and the latter, a slang term, is found in a wide variety of works: the late seventeenth-century manuscript *Purgatorium Hibernicum*, the anonymous comic song "Doran's Ass" and Joyce's *A Portrait of the Artist as a Young Man*. To eliminate such entries on the basis of a narrow view of what constitutes Hiberno-English would not only be questionable on linguistic grounds, it would also reduce the utility of this work considerably.

The realities of Hiberno-English and Anglo-Irish literature make it impossible to establish even the simplest of rules for what to include and exclude, and to apply them consistently. Initially, it seemed reasonable to exclude all words of Hiberno-English origin, such as *colleen*, that are now part of the common currency of the English language, and readily accessible in dictionaries of English. Even that simple rule had to be compromised, because some writers use a variant, *calleen*, or the Irish word, *cailín*, from which *colleen* is derived; and because of the problem of what to do with the common Hiberno-English phrase of endearment, "colleen bawn," which appears in a number of titles and texts: the ballad, "Willy Reilly and the Colleen Bawn"; William Carleton's novel, *Willy Reilly and His Dear Colleen Bawn* (1855); Dion Boucicault's melodrama, *The Colleen Bawn* (1860); and in the text of Sean O'Casey's *Juno and the Paycock*, Joyce's *Ulysses* and *Finnegans Wake*.

The earliest illustrative quotation in this work is taken from Edmund Spenser's *A View of the Present State of Ireland* (ca. 1596) and the most recent is from Roddy Doyle's *The Van* (1991), but the vast majority are from works written in the fifty-year period between 1889, the year in which Yeats's *The Wanderings of Oisin and Other Poems* was published, and 1939, the year of Yeats's death, and the publication of the largest and most significant repository of Hiberno-English in the history of the vernacular, Joyce's *Finnegans Wake*. The occasional quotation from Spenser is used to illustrate the history of a term, and the occasional quotation from Doyle, and others who are obviously not Literary Revival writers, is used to illustrate rare terms in such works as *Finnegans Wake*, where the meaning may not be at all clear. As in the case of the Hiberno-English, I have, for practical reasons, opted for a liberal definition of what constitutes the Irish Literary Revival, by including quotations from the works of all the major and a number of the minor Irish writers who were active in the fifty-year period, 1889-1939. A narrow definition would exclude quotations from such rich sources of Hiberno-English as the works of the Ascendancy writers, Edith Somerville and Martin Ross (Violet Martin), and the Ulster writer, Alexander Irvine, and could lead to the absurdity of excluding Sean O'Casey's controversial play about *An Tostal* (meaning an assembly or pageant, a short-lived, Spring cultural festival started in 1953), *The Drums of Father Ned*, which was first produced in 1959, twenty years after the death of Yeats and the publication of *Finnegans Wake*.

A particular problem facing the compiler of a dictionary such as this is one of several rooted in the unfettered nature of vernaculars. (What is a problem for the compiler may, of course, be a joy for a writer such as Joyce.) That problem is spelling. In the absence of standardized spelling, authors attempt to spell words and phrases phonetically, using ears and an alphabet ill-suited for the purpose. As a result, authors are very inconsistent in their spelling of Hiberno-English. This is particularly true in the case of exclamations and expressions of endearment derived from Irish. It is not uncommon to find three of four variants of a word or phrase in an individual text. Most of these inconsistencies are the result of carelessness; however, in the case of a work such as *Finnegans Wake*, they are conscious and an integral part of the multilingual fabric of the text. In many instances the compiler must find variants scattered across the alphabet and decide under which form to list the main entry if there is no usual form, and this is frequently the case. The exclamation *alilu*, which appears in a wide variety of texts written over a period of three hundred years, from Richard Head's play *Hic et Ubique* (1663) to Benedict Kiely's short story "A Ball of Malt and Madame Butterfly" (1973), has seventeen forms (more are probably lurking around), and must be cross-referenced under its various forms, which begin with the letters f, i, p, u, and w, if the dictionary is to be user-friendly, to use current jargon. I have opted for a radical solution to this vexing problem by simply including all the variants from the Revival period along with all of the variants I have discovered in print. This solution has two obvious advantages: it greatly reduces the chances of a reader encountering a word or phrase in a variant form I have not recorded, and it increases the utility of the work considerably by making it relevant to the entire field of Anglo-Irish literature.

The need for works such as this was articulated as early as 1800 by Maria Edgeworth as "editor" of the narrative of Thady Quirke in *Castle Rackrent*, the first Anglo-Irish novel. In the preface to the glossary appended to the novel, she writes: "Some friends who have seen Thady's history since it has been printed have suggested to the Editor, that many of the terms and idiomatic phrases, with which it abounds, could not be intelligble to the English reader without further explanation."[2] The need which she perceived has increased greatly over the years. Indeed, if she were writing today, she would be obliged to drop the reference to the English reader, because there are now few readers of Anglo-Irish literature, regardless of nationality, who do not, on occasion, require assistance with Hiberno-English. Many rare and obsolete words and phrases in Anglo-Irish literature are now as hermetic to the Irish as they are to the non-Irish reader. There is evidence that Yeats and Joyce, to some extent, shared Edgeworth's concern. Both, on occasion, felt the need to draw attention to and explain their use of Hiberno-English.[3] The need for a work such as this is compounded by the fact that there is, as yet, no dictionary of Hiberno-English to which a reader or writer can turn for assistance.[4] In a discussion of Hiberno-English in "A New Look at the Language Question", the contemporary writer Tom Paulin states: "Until recently no writer has felt frustrated by the absence of a dictionary which might define those words which are in common usage, but which do not appear in the *OED*." The extent of his frustration is revealed in his forceful conclusion: "One of the results of this enormous cultural impoverishment is a living but fragmented speech, an untold number of homeless words, and an uncertain or a derelict prose."[5]

[2] Maria Edgeworth. *Castle Rackrent*. London: Oxford University Press, 1964, p. 98; Edgeworth also provided a glossary in the text of the narrative.
[3] *The Collected Poems of W. B. Yeats* (London: Macmillan and Co. Ltd., 1963), p. 534; *Letters of James Joyce*, 1, ed. Stuart Gilbert (New York: Viking Press, p. 248; *Selected Letters of James Joyce*, ed. Richard Ellmann (London: Faber and Faber, 1975), p. 297.
[4] In 1971 the Royal Irish Academy Committee for the Study of Anglo-Irish Language and Literature announced its intention to begin collecting contributions towards an Anglo-Irish Dictionary (excluding the Ulster dialect, because it presented special problems and required special treatment) and asked for volunteer readers to supply quotations illustrating the history and meaning of words and phases, but the response was disappointing, and the project was eventually abandoned. (International Association for the Study of Anglo-Irish Literature *Newsletter No. 2*, Autumn/Winter 1971).
[5] "A New Look at the Language Question", in *Ireland and the English Crisis* (Newcastle upon Tyne: Blood Axe Books, 1984), p. 191, 192.

In addition to the opinions of writers, there is considerable con-crete evidence of the need for a work such as this in the form of errors in published criticism.[6] If these errors are any indication, the fact that Hiberno-English causes many problems for those who are unfamiliar with it is not generally recognized. These problems range from incomplete understanding to complete misunderstanding of parts of works. The apparent proximity of Hiberno-English to stan-dard English leads the unsuspecting to take it for granted, and not realize that many words and phrases in Anglo-Irish literature, such as *west* and *wet and dry*, which appear to be standard English are, in certain uses, Hiberno-English.

[6] See my "Joyce's Use of the Anglo-Irish Dialect of English", in Andrew Carpenter, ed., *Place, Personality and the Irish Writer* (Gerrards Cross: Colin Smythe; New York: Barnes and Noble, 1977), p. 121; and "Dialect in Irish Literature: The Hermetic Core" in *The Irish University Review*, vol. 20, no. 1, Spring 1990, 8–18.

A CHRONOLOGY OF AUTHORS QUOTED

Spenser, Edmund	ca. 1552-1599
Edgeworth, Maria	1767-1849
Maxwell, William Hamilton	1792-1850
Carleton, William	1794-1869
Lover, Samuel	1797-1868
Griffin, Gerald	1803-1840
Mangan, James Clarence	1803-1849
Ferguson, Samuel	1810-1886
Boucicault, Dion	ca. 1820-1890
Joyce, Patrick Weston	1827-1914
Moore, George	1852-1933
O'Crohan, Tomás	1856-1937
Shaw, George Bernard	1856-1950
Somerville, E. Œ.	1858-1949
Gregory, Augusta	1859-1932
Irvine, Alexander	ca. 1869-1941
Hyde, Douglas	1860-1949
Ross, Martin (pseud. of Violet Martin)	1861-1915
Yeats, William Butler	1865-1939
A.E. (pseud. of George W. Russell)	1867-1935
Synge, John Millington	1871-1909
Sayers, Peig	1873-1958
O'Kelly, Seumas	ca. 1875-1918
Fitzmaurice, George	ca. 1877-1963
Gogarty, Oliver, St John	1878-1957
Corkery, Daniel	1878-1964
Pearse, Patrick	1879-1916
Campbell, Joseph	1879-1944
Colum, Padraic	1881-1972
Joyce, James	1882-1941
O'Casey, Sean	1884-1964
Ledwidge, Francis	1887-1917
MacNamara, Brinsley (pseud. of John Weldon)	1890-1963

O'Connor, Frank (pseud. of Michael O'Donovan)	1903-1966
Cross, Eric	ca. 1903-1980
Beckett, Samuel	1906-1989
O'Brien, Flann (pseud. of Brian O'Nolan)	1911-1966
Macken, Walter	1915-1967
Behan, Brendan	1923-1964
Flanagan, Thomas	1924-
Leonard, Hugh (pseud. of John Keyes Byrne)	1926-
Keane, John B.	1928-
Friel, Brian	1929-
McCabe, Eugene	1930-
Dunne, Lee	1934-
Murphy, Thomas	1935-
MacLaverty, Bernard	1942-
Doyle, Roddy	1958-

AUTHORS AND WORKS QUOTED

A.E., *P*: A.E. (George Russell). *Collected Poems*. London: Macmillan and Co., 1913.

——, *U*: ——. "Upon an Airy Upland", in *The Mentor Book of Irish Poetry*. Ed. Devin A. Garrity. Toronto: The New American Library of Canada, 1965.

Beckett, *M*: Samuel Beckett. *More Pricks Than Kicks*. New York: Grove Press, 1972.

——, *MU*: ——. *Murphy*. London: Pan Books, 1973.

Behan, *H*: Brendan Behan. *The Hostage*, in *An Giall* (trans., ed. Richard Wall) *and The Hostage* (ed. Richard Wall). Washington, D.C.: The Catholic University of America Press; Gerrards Cross, Colin Smythe, 1987.

——, *W*: ——. *After the Wake*. Dublin: The O'Brien Press, 1987.

Boucicault, *C*: Dion Boucicault. *Arrah-na-Pogue*, in *The Dolmen Boucicault*. Ed. David Krause. Dublin: The Dolmen Press, 1964.

Campbell, *P*: Joseph Campbell. *Poems of Joseph Campbell*. Dublin: Allen Figgis, 1963.

Carleton, *S*: William Carleton. *Stories From Carleton*. Intro. W. B. Yeats. London: Walter Scott, n.d.

Colum, *PC*: Padraic Colum. *The Poet's Circuits: Collected Poems of Ireland*. Dublin: The Dolmen Press, 1981.

——, *PO*: ——. *Poems*. London: Macmillan and Co., 1932.

Corkery, *D*: Tom Corkery. *Tom Corkery's Dublin*. Dublin: Anvil Books, 1980.

Corkery, *H*: Daniel Corkery. *The Hounds of Banba*. Dublin: The Talbot Press, 1920.

——, *I*: ——. *I Bhreasail*. London: Elkin Mathews, 1921.

——, *M*: ——. *A Munster Twilight*. Dublin: The Talbot Press, 1916.

——, *S*: ——. *The Stormy Hills*. Dublin: The Talbot Press, n.d.

Crosbie, *D*: Paddy Crosbie. *Your Dinner's Poured Out*. Dublin: The O'Brien Press, 1981.

Cross, *T*: Eric Cross. *The Tailor and Ansty*. Cork: The Mercier Press, 1975.

Doyle, *V*: Roddy Doyle. *The Van*. London: Secker and Warburg, 1991.

Dunne, *G*: Lee Dunne. *Goodbye to the Hill*. Dublin: Wolfhound Press, 1986.

Ferguson, *P*: Samuel Ferguson. *The Poems of Samuel Ferguson*. Dublin: Allen Figgis, 1963.

Fitzmaurice, *F*: George Fitzmaurice. *The Plays of George Fitzmaurice: Dramatic Fantasies*. Dublin: The Dolmen Press, 1967.

——, *R*: ——. *The Plays of George Fitzmaurice: Realistic Plays*. Dublin: The Dolmen Press, 1970.

Flanagan, *T*: Thomas Flanangan. *The Tenants of Time*. New York: Warner Books, 1989.

Friel, *P*: Brian Friel. *Philadelphia, Here I Come!* in *Selected Plays of Brian Friel*. London: Faber and Faber, 1984.

——, *T*: ——. *Translations*. *Ibid*.

Gogarty, *A*: Oliver St J. Gogarty. *As I Was Going Down Sackville Street*. Harmondsworth: Penguin Books, 1954.

Gregory, *B*: Lady Gregory. *The Blessed Trinity of Ireland*. Gerrards Cross: Colin Smythe, 1985.

——, *P*: ——. *Poets and Dreamers*. Gerrards Cross: Colin Smythe, 1974.

——, *SP*: ——. *Selected Plays*. London: Putnam and Co., 1962.

Griffin, *H*: Gerald Griffin. "Hy-Brasail", in *The Mentor Book of Irish Poetry*. Ed. Devin A. Garrity. Toronto: The New American Library of Canada, 1965.

Hyde, *L*: Douglas Hyde. *Love Songs of Connacht*. Shannon: Irish University Press, 1969.

——, *R*: ——. "Rann," in *The Mentor Book of Irish Poetry*. Ed. Devin A. Garrity. Toronto: The New American Library of Canada, 1965.

——, *T*: ——. *The Twisting of the Rope*, in Lady Gregory. *Poets and Dreamers*. Gerrards Cross: Colin Smythe, 1974.

——, *S*: ——. *The Tinker and the Sheeog*. *Ibid*.

Irvine, *L*: Alexander Irvine. *My Lady of the Chimney Corner*. Belfast: The Appletree Press, 1980.

Joyce, *CW*: James Joyce. *The Critical Writings of James Joyce*. Ed. Ellsworth Mason and Richard Ellmann. New York: Viking Press, 1959.

——, *D*: ——. *Dubliners*. New York: Viking Press, 1969.

——, *E*: ——. *Exiles*. New York: Viking Press, 1951.

Joyce, *ESI*: P. W. Joyce. *English as we speak it in Ireland*. London: Longmans, Greene and Co.; Dublin, M. H. Gill, 1910.

Joyce, *FW*: James Joyce. *Finnegans Wake*. New York: Viking Press, 1959.

——, *L, I*: ——. *Letters of James Joyce, I*. Ed. Stuart Gilbert. New York: Viking Press, 1966.

——, *P*: ——. *A Portrait of the Artist as a Young Man*. New York: Viking Press, 1964.

——, *SH*: ——. *Stephen Hero*. New York: New Directions, 1963.

——, *U*: ——. *Ulysses*. New York: Random House, 1961.

Keane, *MY*: John B. Keane. *Many Young Men of Twenty*. Dublin: Progress House Publications, 1961.

Ledwidge, *B*: Francis Ledwidge. "The Blackbirds", in *The Penguin Book of Irish Verse*. Ed. Brendan Kennelly. Harmondsworth: Penguin Books, 1970.

——, *M*: ——. "Thomas McDonagh", *ibid*.

Leonard, *D*: Hugh Leonard. *Da*, in *Da, A Life and Time Was*. Harmondsworth: Penguin Books, 1981.

——, *H*: ——. *Home Before Night*. Harmondsworth: Penguin Books, 1981.

——, *O*: ——. *Out After Dark*. Harmondsworth: Penguin Books, 1990.

Lover, *L*: Samuel Lover. *Legends and Stories of Ireland*. Boston: Little, Brown and Co., 1902.

McCabe, *C*: Eugene McCabe. "Cancer", in *Modern Irish Short Stories*. Ed. Ben Forkner. Harmondsworth: Penguin Books, 1980.

Macken, *SW*: Walter Macken. *The Scorching Wind*. London: Pan Books, 1981.

MacLaverty, *S*: Bernard MacLaverty. "Some Surrender", in "Weekend", a supplement to *The Irish Times*. Dublin: Saturday 8 August, 1987.

MacMahon, *H*: Bryan MacMahon. *The Honey Spike*. London: Arrow Books, 1989.

MacNamara, *V*: Brinsley MacNamara. *The Valley of the Squinting Windows*. London: Sampson Low, Marston and Co., n.d.

Mangan, *P*: James Clarence Mangan. *Poems of James Clarence Mangan*. Ed. D. J. O'Donoghue. Dublin: M. H. Gill and Son, 1922.

Maxwell, *W*: W. H. Maxwell. *Wild Sports of the West*. Dublin: The Talbot Press, n.d.

Moore, *M*: George Moore. *Muslin*. London: William Heinemann and Sons, 1936.

——, *H*: ——. "Home Sickness", in *Modern Irish Short Stories*. Ed. Ben Forkner. Harmondsworth: Penguin Books, 1980.

Murphy, *C*: Thomas Murphy. *A Crucial Week in the Life of a Grocer's Assistant*. Dublin: Gallery Press, 1979.

——, *F:* ——. *Famine.* Dublin: Gallery Press, 1986.

O'Brien, *H:* Flann O'Brien. *The Hard Life.* London: Pan Books, 1976.

O'Casey, *A, I & II:* Sean O'Casey. *Autobiographies, I & II.* London, Macmillan and Co., 1963.

——, *B:* ——. *The Bishop's Bonfire,* in *Seven Plays by Sean O'Casey.* Ed. Ronald Ayling. Basingstoke: Macmillan Publishers, 1985.

——, *D:* ——. *The Drums of Father Ned.* London: Macmillan and Co., 1960.

——, *H:* ——. *The Harvest Festival.* New York: The New York Public Library; Gerrards Cross: Colin Smythe, 1979.

——, *J,* ——. *Juno and the Paycock,* in *Seven Plays by Sean O'Casey.* Ed. Ronald Ayling. Basingstoke: Macmillan Publishers, 1985.

——, *P:* ——. *The Plough and the Stars. Ibid.*

——, *R:* ——. *Red Roses for Me. Ibid.*

——, *S:* ——. *The Shadow of a Gunman, Ibid.*

O'Connor, *O:* Frank O'Connor. *My Oedipus Complex and Other Stories.* Harmondsworth: Penguin Books, 1986.

O'Crohan, *I:* Tomás O'Crohan. *Island Cross-Talk.* Trans. Tim Enright. Oxford: Oxford University Press, 1986.

——, *IM:* ——. *The Islandman.* Trans. Robin Flower. Oxford: The Clarendon Press, 1958.

O'Kelly, *H:* Seumas O'Kelly. *Hillsiders.* Dublin: The Talbot Press, n.d.

Pearse, *P:* Patrick Pearse. *Plays, Stories, Poems.* Dublin: The Talbot Press, 1958.

Redmond, *S:* Lar Redmond. *Show Us The Moon.* Dingle, Co. Kerry: Brandon Book Publishers, 1988.

Sayers, *P:* Peig Sayers. *Peig.* Trans. Bryan MacMahon. Dublin: The Talbot Press, 1983.

Shaw, *J:* Bernard Shaw. *John Bull's Other Island,* in *The Complete Plays of Bernard Shaw.* London: Paul Hamlyn, 1965.

Somerville and Ross, *A:* E. Œ. Somerville and Martin Ross. *All on the Irish Shore.* London: Longmans, Green, and Co., 1903.

——, *B:* ——. *The Big House of Inver.* London: The Zodiac Press, 1973.

——, *RM:* ——. *Some Experiences of an Irish R.M.* London: Longmans, Green, and Co., 1905.

——, *RME:* ——. *The Irish R.M. and his Experiences.* London: Faber and Faber, 1928.

Spenser, *V:* Edmund Spenser. *A View of the Present State of Ireland.* Ed. W. L. Renwick. Oxford: The Clarendon Press, 1970.

Synge, *A:* J. M. Synge. *The Aran Islands,* in *J. M. Synge Collected Works, II* (Prose). Ed. Alan Price. London: Oxford University Press, 1966; Gerrards Cross: Colin Smythe, 1982.

——, D: ——. *Deirdre of the Sorrows*, in J. M. Synge *Collected Works, IV* (Plays II). Ed. Ann Saddlemeyer. London: Oxford University Press, 1968; Gerrards Cross: Colin Smythe, 1982.

——, P: —. *The Playboy of the Western World. Ibid.*

——, PO: ——. *Poems*, in J. M. Synge *Collected Works, 1* (Poems). Ed. Robin Skelton. London: Oxford University Press, 1962; Gerrards Cross: Colin Smythe, 1982.

——, R: ——. *Riders to the Sea*, in J. M. Synge *Collected Works, III* (Plays I). Ed. Ann Saddlemeyer. London: Oxford University Press, 1968; Gerrards Cross: Colin Smythe, 1982.

——, S: ——. *The Shadow of the Glen. Ibid.*

Yeats, PL: W. B. Yeats. *The Collected Plays of W. B. Yeats*. London: Macmillan and Co., 1960.

——, PO: ——. *The Collected Poems of W. B. Yeats*. London: Macmillan and Co., 1963.

——, M: ——. *Mythologies*. London: Macmillan and Co., 1962.

Yeats and Gregory, U: Katherine Worth, ed. *Where There Is Nothing/The Unicorn from the Stars*. Washington, D.C.: The Catholic University of America Press; Gerrards Cross: Colin Smythe, 1987.

ABBREVIATIONS

a.	adjective	Ir.	Irish (Gaelic)
A.F.	Anglo-French	iron.	ironic
A.I.	Anglo-Irish	L.	Latin
abbr.	abbreviation	lit.	literary
ad.	adverb	M.E.	Middle English
anon.	anonymous	M.I.	Middle Irish
Ap.	Appendix	met.	metaphor
b.	born	ms.	manuscript
Br.	British	mod.	modern
c.	century	N.	northern
c. phr.	catch phrase	n.	noun
ca.	*circa*	nic.	nickname
col.	colloquial	obs.	obsolete
com.	common	occ.	occasionally
comb.	combination	O.E.	Old English
cur.	current	orig.	originally
d.	died	pej.	pejorative
Dan.	Danish	perh.	perhaps
dial.	dialect	phr.	phrase
dim.	diminutive	pl.	plural
Dub.	Dublin	pr.	pronoun
emph.	emphatic	pre.	prefix
end.	endearment	prep.	preposition
Engl.	Modern English	pron.	pronunciation
esp.	especially	prov.	proverb
estd.	established	quot.	quotation
euph.	euphemism	s. phr.	stock phrase
excl.	exclamation	sal.	salutation
expl.	expletive	Sc.	Scots
folk.	folklore	sl.	slang
Fr.	French	slog.	slogan
H.E.	Hiberno-English	st.	stanza
hist.	historical	suf.	suffix
interj.	interjection	Uls.	Ulster

usu.	usual (usually)	var.	variant
v.	verb	voc.	vocative

KEY TO DICTIONARY AND GLOSSARY

An entry may have up to nine parts:

1.   The word or phrase (listed in alphabetical order according to the usual spelling or form, if such there be).
2.   If there are variants, they appear in brackets following the usual spelling or form. To increase the utility of the work, the variants are drawn from the entire range of Anglo-Irish literature. Each variant is also listed alphabetically and directs the reader to the main entry.
3.   The grammatical and/or rhetorical function of the entry.
4.   Definition.
5.   If the entry has any connotations, or is associated with a particular place or region, that information is given in brackets at the end of the definition (The identification of an idiom with a particular location does not imply that it is confined to that location).
6.   The etymology of the word, or source of the phrase, is given, if it is known. The meaning of an Irish word or phrase appearing in this part is not given when it coincides with the meaning in Hiberno-English.
7.   An illustrative quotation or quotations and source(s). In some instances, particularly in cases of rare Hiberno-English located in Joyce's *Finnegans Wake* where the meaning is not at all clear, the illustrative quotations may be taken from works outside the Revival period.
8.   If an illustrative quotation contains additional Hiberno-English to that under consideration, or if an entry is related to another entry or entries, the user is directed to the appropriate entry or entries.
9.   If an entry has any particular literary, historical or social significance, or is used in the title of a work, that information is given in the glossary at the end of the entry.

PRONUNCIATION GUIDE

The high incidence of variant forms for the entries in this work is, to a large extent, a reflection of the fact that there is a very wide geographic and social range of pronunciations in Hiberno-English, and no generally accepted standard. Bearing this in mind, the following is a simple guide to the pronunciation of words most likely to cause problems for those unfamiliar with H.E. (stressed syllables italicized).

aingisheoir	*ang* a shore
aisling	*ash* ling
ardri	*ard* ree
Arragowan	Are a go wan
Arrah	Are ah
asthora	a store a
bacach	baw *cock*
badhach	bow dock
bairneach	bar knock
bannalanna	ban a lan na
Bealtaine	*Bail* te ne
beannacht	ban nacht
bonham	*bon* am
bouchal	boo a cal
buddaree	*bud* are ree
cailleach	kal yock
caman	ka mawn
caoine	key ne
ciarog	kiar ogue
cnawvshawl	knov shawl
cnuceen	*knuck* een
Dail	Doyle
dearg	*dar* ag
dhiol	dee owl
dhu	do

Eire	Eh reh
failte	foil che
feis	fesh
Fodhla	Foh la
gardai	gar dee
garradhuv	gar a dove
gra	graw
Grainne	*Grawn* neh
Granuaile	Graw new wale
grianaun	green awn
gwal	go *wal*
inagh	in *yah*
Inisfail	In ish foil
Iosa	*E* o sa
lannan shee	lan awn she
laogh	lay
leaca	*lack* a
leathan	la han
lebidin	le be deen
oinseach	owen shuck
oireachtas	ir ock tas
ollamh	ol av
omadhaun	om a dawn
pastheeen	pash teen
pishog	pish ogue
plamais	plaw maws
poirse	pour sha
praties	pray tees
raimeis	raw maysh
rinnce	*rink* a
Róisín	Ro sheen
Samhain	Sow an
segocia	se go sha
shanachie	shan a key
shaughran	shag rawn
shoneen	show neen
siabhra	seev ra
Sinn Fein	Shin Fain
slainte	slawn cha
spailpin	spol peen
tanist	taw nist
Taoiseach	Tea shock

Tir na nOg	Tear na nogue
Tostal	Tow stal
usquebaugh	ish ka ba
wirrasthrue	wir as true

DICTIONARY AND GLOSSARY

aboo (abo, abu) *excl.* to victory; for ever. [< Ir. *abú*.] Joyce, *FW*, 372.25: "Boree aboo!" Corkery, *H*, 46: "Sinn Fein abu! — and high time too!" See: Sinn Fein. ["O'Donnell Aboo" is a popular marching song by Michael Joseph McCann (1824-1883), which was adopted as a signature tune by Radió Éireann; the wrenboys set out to its strains in *The Bodhrán Makers* (1986), a novel by John B. Keane (1928-); "*Crom (God) Aboo!*" is the slog. of the Fitzgerald family, and *Lámh Dearg* (Red Hand of Ulster) *Abú* is that of the O'Neill family.]

absentee see: rack (rack-rent).

abu see: aboo.

ace see: aim's ace.

ach see: och.

achone see: ochone.

achora (achorra, a-chorra, a-chára, a chara) *voc., n.* my friend (end.); a sal. in letters. [< Ir. *a chara*.] Joyce, *U*, 296: "Never better, *a chara*, says he." Corkery, *D*, 32: "He . . . foams at the mouth every time he sees a uniform or gets a letter describing him as *A Chara*." [*A Chara* is sometimes used instead of the sal., Dear Sir or Madam, in formal letters written in Engl. after independence, particularly those of government departments and agencies, as a gesture towards the use of Ir., because the state is, officially, bilingual. For the same reason, the plural, *A Chairde*, is sometimes used instead of the sal., Ladies and Gentlemen, at the beginning of speeches. John B. Keane ridicules this practice, particularly by those who do not know Ir., in his play *Many Young Men of Twenty* (1961): "A Chairde Ghael! O, Uh, Gu, Bo, Boola. Bo, Wo, Bow Wow! I always believe in a few words in Irish first" (39). The practice of lip service to Ir., very common among politicians, is sometimes derisively called giving the "*cúpla focal*" (a few words).]

achree see: machree.

achudth (a chuid) *voc., n.* my dear (end.). [<Ir. *a chuid*.] Somerville and Ross, *RM*, 178: "[D]on't be unaisy, achudth; he's doing grand." Pearse, *P*, 263: "She not, *a chuid*."

acting the goat (maggot)   *c. phr.* behaving in a deliberately foolish or obtuse manner. O'Casey, *D*, 73: "[S]o don't be actin' th' goat . . . ." ["Acting the Maggot" is a chapter in Bob Geldolf's autobiography, *Is That It?* (1986).]

acushla (acuishla, a chuisle, a cuishla, cuishla, cushla, cushleen, cushlamachree, macushla)   *voc., n.* my darling (end.). [< Ir. *a (mo) chuisle*, o (my) pulse (of my heart).] Joyce, *U*, 600: "Remove him, acushla." Pearse, *P*, 265: "I did, *a chuisle*." ["Acushala Gal Machree" is a song; an adaptation of *Guy Mannering* (1815), a novel by Sir Walter Scott (1771-1832), for the stage by Dion Boucicault is entitled *Cushla-Machree* (1888); "Macushla" is a love song made famous by the Irish tenor John McCormack (1884-1945); *The Blue Macushla* (1980) is a play by Thomas Murphy (1935-); there is a pun on the term in Joyce's *Finnegans Wake*: "one cushlin his crease" (136.03).]

adzehead   *nic.* an early Christian missionary to Ireland; from the fancied resemblance between the shape of an adze, and a bearded face and tonsured head. Gregory, *B*, 52: "Adzeheads will come over an angry sea; their cloaks hole-headed; their staves crooked; their tables to the east of their houses; they will answer Amen." [Shem the Penman in Joyce's *Finnegans Wake* has "an adze of a skull" (161.11).]

agra (agradh, agrah, aghra, a'ra, gra, gradh, gradh geal, gragh, grah, graw, agragil)   *voc., n.* my (bright) love (end.). [< Ir. *a ghrádh (geal)*, my (bright) love.] O'Casey, *B*, 484: "Thanks, Foorawn, agradh . . . ." Joyce, *FW*, 358.32: ". . . The two Gemuas and Jane Agrah . . . ." *Ibid.*, 317.36: "[H]e was . . . still trystfully acape for his gragh. . . ." Fitzmaurice, *F*, 22: "[H]e has such a grah for a dandy doll. . . ." *Ibid.*, 79: "Faith, he can't, agragil. . . ." Corkery, *H*, 102: "I am winging to my *gradh geal*, to my bright love . . . ." ["Gra Gal Machree" is a song.]

aililiu   see: alilu.

aim's ace (aims-ace, ace)   *n.* a minute distance. [< M.E. *ambs* (double) *as* (ace), the lowest possible throw in the game of dice.] Joyce, *P*, 182: "One of the two Crokes made a woeful wipe [sic] at him one time with his camann and I declare to God he was within an aim's ace of getting it at the side of the temple." Irvine, *L*, 95: "I was jist within an ace ov goin' over an' pullin' ye out be th' heels myself." See: wipe, camann.

aingisheoir (angashore, anghashore)   *n.* a poor, miserable person. [< Ir. *ainniseoir*.] Fitzmaurice, *F*, 46: "[W]hat's pinching my old angashore not be making a move?" Fitzmaurice, *R*, 90: "[T]hat same Bridie would marry an oldish man for his cash an make a cuckold of him, like Maureen-so-fine and her poor old anghashore of a husband. . . ."

airt see: art.

airy *a.* haunted, eerie, fearsome. [< Ir. *aerach.*] A.E., *U*, 23: "Upon an airy upland / Within me and far away / A child that's ageless dances / All delicately gay. A dance that is like sunshine / While I am old and grey." ["Upon an Airy Upland" is a poem by A.E. (George Russell, in which the poet is haunted by the ghost of his youth.]

aisling (aislinn) *n.* a dream, a vision; a vision poem (lit.); popular in recent years as a name for girls. [Ir. *aisling.*] Joyce, *FW*, 179.31: "[E]very splurge on the vellum he blundered over was an aisling vision more gorgeous than the one before. . . ." Colum, *PO*, 22: "It is strange to name / Anyone in the world Aislinn: Dream." [The aisling was a popular Gaelic form in the 18th c., especially in Munster. The poet dreams and has a vision of a fair lady, Ireland, who tells him the good news that Ireland will be delivered from the misery of English rule and the Catholic Stuarts will return to the throne. The most famous aisling is the satiric, bawdy and controversial, *Cúirt an Mhean Oíche* (*The Midnight Court*), by Brian Merriman (ca. 1747-1805). It is over 1,000 lines long and has been translated into English by writers such as Percival Arland Ussher (preface by W. B. Yeats), Frank O'Connor and Lord Longford. The form influenced modern Irish poetry. "The *Aisling*" is a chapter in *The Hidden Ireland* (1924) by Daniel Corkery; "Aisling" is a poem by Austin Clarke (1896-1974), and a play (1953) by Maurice Meldon (1926-1958).]

alanna (a lanna, alannah, allanna, alainia, lanna, ma lanuv, ma llanuv, lanv, leanav) *voc., n.* my child, my darling (end.). [< Ir. *a (mo) leanbh.*] O'Casey, *J*, 71: "An' what is it you're thinkin' of, allanna?" Joyce, *FW*, 330.07: " 'Twere yeg will elsecare doatty lanv meet they dewsent hyemn to cannons' roar and rifles peal vill shantey soloweys sang!" [The quot. from Joyce's *Finnegans Wake* contains a parody of the last line of the chorus of "A Soldier's Song," the Irish national anthem, words of which were composed by Peadar Kearney (1883-1942), uncle of Brendan Behan: " 'Mid cannon's roar and rifles peal,/ We'll chant a soldier's song." "Eileen Alannah" is a sentimental song.]

Alba (Alban) *n.* Scotland (lit.). [Ir. *Alba.*] Yeats, *PL*, 276: "A soldier out of Alba?" Synge, *D*, 213: "My two brothers, I am going with Naisi to Alban and the north, to face the troubles are foretold."

alilu (allilu, aililiu, fuillilaloo, illilo, phillelew, phillilew, pillaloo, pillalu, pillilew, pilliloo, pullaloo, ullaloo, ul-ullalu, ulalu, ullalu, whillaluh) *excl., interj., n.* alas; a cry of distress. [< Ir. *aililiú,* or*fuilibilis,* or *puillilliú.*] Sayers, *P*, 88: "*Aililiú!* . . . What's goin'

on here?" Somerville and Ross, *RM*, 294: ". . . Pillilew! What's this?"
Yeats, *PO*, 19: "[L]ift a mournful ulalu, / For the kind wires are
torn and still . . . ."
amac see: avic.
amadan see: omadhaun.
American wake see: convey.
amhran see: avran.
amirra see: wirra.
amplush (namplush) *n.*, *v.* dilemma, difficulty or disadvantage.
[Perh. < Ir. *amplais*, jeopardy or dilemma; or a var. of nonplus.]
Carleton, *S*, 35: "Now may I be shot wid a blank cartridge if I ever
felt so much at an amplush in my life . . . ." Lover, *L*, 173: "[O]nly
I'm aiqual to a counsellor for knowledge, he'd have namplushed me
long ago." [The word is the basis of a pun in Joyce's *Finnegans Wake*:
"[T]he man . . . up from the bog of the depths who was raging
with the thirst . . . , was only standing there nonplush to the corner
of Turbot Street, perplexing about a paumpshop . . ." (516.27).]
anamon dhoul see: manim an diouol.
Andrew Martins (anthrimartins, antrumartins) *n.* *(pl.)* pranks,
tricks. Joyce, *FW*, 392.03: "[S]ure, he was only funning with his
andrewmartins. . . ." O'Casey, *D*, 31: "Why don't yous pick out
McGilligan's house for your anthrimartins.?" [In the Joyce quot.
there may be a pun on martheen, a stocking with the foot cut off
(< Ir. *mairtín*); the term Andrew Martins also appears, lightly disguised, in *Finnegans Wake*: "[T]imkin abeat your Andraws Meltons
and his lovesang of the short and shifty . . ." (328:05-06).]
angashore see: aingisheoir.
anthrimartins (antrumartins) see: Andrew Martins.
Ara (Arah) see: Arrah.
ardri *n.* high king (lit.). [Ir. *árd rí*.] Joyce, *U*, 296: "From his
girdle hung a row of seastones . . . and on these were graven . . . the
tribal images of many of the Irish heroes and heroines of antiquity,
Cuchulin, Conn of the hundred battles, Niall of the nine hostages,
Brian of Kincora, the Ardri Malachi . . . ."
aroo see: aru.
aroon (a-roon, roon, a ruin) *voc.*, *n.* my darling, beloved (end.,
lit.). [< Ir. *a rúin*.] O'Casey, *J*, 69: "Who was it led the van, Soggart
Aroon? / Since the fight first began, Soggart Aroon?" Hyde, *L*, 135:
"She is my roon, oh, she my roon, / Who tells me nothing, leaves
me soon . . . ." Pearse, *P*, 263: "What is it *a rúin*." See: Soggart.
["Peggy Aroon" and "Shule Aroon" are songs; "Soggarth Aroon"
is a patriotic song by the novelist John Banim (1798-1842); " Eileen
Aroon" is a love song by the novelist Gerald Griffin (1803-1840),

Aileen Aroon (1870) is a novel by Charles Anderson Read (1841-1878); Miss Aroon St. Charles is the narrator of *Good Behaviour* (1981), a novel by Molly Keane (1905-): *Eileen O'Roon* is a play by Ernest Gebler (1915-).]

Arragowan   *interj.* expostulatory or deprecatory, used at the beginning of a statement. [Comb. of arrah + go + on.] Beckett, *M*, 46: " 'Arragowan' she said 'make it four cantcher, yer frien', yer da, yer ma an' yer motte.' " See: arrah, mot (motte).

Arrah (Ara, Arah, Erra, Errah, Orra, Yerra, Yerrah, Yarra, Yarrah, Yirrah)   *interj.* But, Now, Really: expostulatory or deprecatory, used at the beginning of a statement; erra is rare, arrah and yerra are equally com. but yerra is slightly more emph. [< Ir. *ara*, same meaning; often preceded by *a Dhia*, (O God) and the whole contracted to *Dheara* (Yerra in H.E.).] Moore, *M*, 104: "An Englishman here! . . . Arrah! he'll go back quicker than he came." Pearse, *P*, 105: "Ara, shut up, yourself . . . ." Joyce, *FW*, 6.13: "Macool, Macool, orra whyi deed ye diie?" Joyce, *D*, 127: "Yerra, sure the little hop-o'-my-thumb has forgotten all about it." Somerville and Ross, *A*, 256: "Yirrah, what dhrag man!" [Arrah-na-Pogue (of the Kiss) is the heroine of *Arrah-na-Pogue* (1864), a play by Dion Boucicault; "Arrah! will you marry me" is a song; Arrah O'Donnell is the heroine of *Mistress of the Eagles* (1990), a novel based on the life of Grace O'Malley (Granuaile, ca.1530-1603), by the Canadian writer Elona Malterre; see: Granuaile.]

art (airt)   *n.* direction (Uls.). [Perh. < Ir. *áird*, direction, point of the compass.] Pearse, *P*, 212: "People were making on the spot from every art." [Com. in Sc, and in the s. phr., "from all arts and parts".]

artist   *a., n.* rogue, poseur (pej.). Joyce, *U*, 38: "Did you see anything of your artist brother Stephen lately?" Gogarty, *A*, 299: " 'A great artist!' he exclaimed, using 'artist' in the sense that it has in Dublin of a quaint fellow or a great cod: a pleasant and unhypocritical poseur, one who sacrifices his own dignity for his friends' diversion." See: cod. [As the quot. from Joyce's *Ulysses* indicates, Stephen Dedalus in *A Portrait of the Artist as a Young Man* and *Ulysses* is something of an artist in the H.E. sense of the word; one of the abusive names HCE is called in Joyce's *Finnegans Wake* is "*Artist*" (71.21).]

aru (aroo, eroo)   *interj.* ah, so, indeed, really. [Ir. *arú*.] O'Crohan, *I*, 58: "Aroo, little hussy, isn't it thinner I'm getting." Joyce, *FW*, 558.29: "[O]ur moddereeen ru [Ir, little fox] arue rue. . . ." See: een, rua (rue).

Ascendancy, the   *n.* the ruling class in Ireland prior to independence. Joyce, *U*, 402: "[H]e had resolved to purchase in fee simple for

ever the freehold of Lambay island from its holder, lord Talbot de
Malahide, a Tory gentleman of not[e] much in favour with our
ascendancy party." Cf. quality, the [*Ascendancy* (1935) is a play
by Lord Longford (1902-1961); "Ascendancy" is a poem by Derry
Jeffares; *Ascendancy and Tradition in Anglo-Irish Literature 1789
to 1939* (1985) is a study by William McCormack (1947-).]

ass's bawl (the bray of an ass), within an   *c. phr.* reasonably close,
or some distance away (depending on context); within earshot of
a braying ass. Behan, *W*, 41:"[T] he buttons were the size of saucers,
or within the bawl of an ass of it . . . ." Joyce, *FW*, 154.01: "How
do you do it? cheeped the Gripes in a wherry whiggy maudelenian
woice and the jackasses all within bawl laughed and brayed for his
intentions. . . ." [In ancient Ireland distance was often measured
vaguely by how far a particular sound, such as the crow of a cock
or the sound of a bell, would travel.]

asthora (asthore, asthoreen, a stoir, astoir, astore, store, storeen,
stooreen, storreen)   *voc., n.* my treasure, my darling (end.). (< Ir.
a stór (ín).] Joyce, *FW*, 397.05: "And there she was right enough,
that lovely sight enough, the girleen bawn asthore, as for days galore,
of planxty Gregory." Somerville and Ross, *B*, 257: "Where's the
sisther, asthoreen?" Hyde, *L*, 135: "She is my store, oh, she is my
store, / Whose grey eye wounded me so sore . . . ." Colum, *PO*,
65: "[T] he cuckoo cries until dark / Where my *storeen* has her bed!"
See: een, bawn 1, planxty. [There is an obvious allusion to Augusta
Gregory in the Joyce quot. "Molly Asthore" is a song, and poem
by Samuel Ferguson.]

asthru   see: wirrasthrue.

astoir (astore)   see: asthora.

augh   see: och.

avic (avich, avick, a vic, a-vich, a vich-o, a mhic, amac, mac)   *voc.,*
n. my boy, my son, son (end.). [< Ir. *a mhic*, my son, or *mac*, a
son.] O'Casey, *R*, 274: "Here y'are, Ayamonn, me son, avic's th'
Irish magazines I got me friend to pinch for you."

avouchal   see: bouchal.

avourneen   see: mavourneen.

avran (amhran)   *n.* a song; a binding set of lines, or concluding stan-
za which recapitulates a poem. [< Ir. *amhrán.*] Corkery, *M*, 80:
"[T] he sorrow that has made us desolate has this night given birth
to a song that will live for ever; because of it my name and your
name and our son's name, which are woven into its amhran meter,
will not pass . . . ." [*Amhrán na bhFiann* is the Ir. title of "A Soldier's
Song," the Irish national anthem.]

away   *euph.* stolen by, or under the spell of, the fairies. Gregory,

P, 90: "The *Lusmor* is the only one that's good to bring back children that are '*away*.' " See: luss (lusmor); cf. them, gentle folk, silly. [This euph. is a manifestation of a universal reluctance to name things that are feared.]

baan see: bawn, 1, 2.

bacach (baccah, bachach, bocach, boccagh, boccah, bococh, bocock, bucaugh) *n.*, *a.* a lame person; a beggar, since many beggars were, or pretended to be, lame (occ. pej.). [Ir. *bacach*.] Gregory, *P*, 36: "[H]e brought all the *bacach* and poor men of Ireland, and gave them a pound each." Campbell, *P*, 62: "All know me only the Stranger, / Who sits on the Saxon's Height: / He burned the bachach's little house / On last St. Brigid's Night." Yeats, *M*, 234: "Every evening the bocachs and beggars and blind men and fiddlers would gather into the house . . . ." Fitzmaurice, *R*, 55: "Ah, look at the mountainy bococh catching him by the tail of the coat and whispering lies into his ears." [Conn Bacach O'Neill (ca. 1484-1599) was the first of the O'Neills to emerge as a leader of the Irish in the struggle against the English in the 16th c.; "Ould Bocock's mare" has an important role in the short story, "Lisheen Races, Second-Hand", by E. Œ. Somerville and Martin Ross; Pats Bocock is a lame tinker in *Sive* (1959/1985), a play by John B. Keane.]

back *n.* an ally in faction fights. [Perh. < Ir. *baicle*, a crowd, a band of workmen.] Yeats, *PL*, 79: "I do be thinking sometimes, now things are going so well with us, and the Cashels such a good back to us in the district . . . ." [Fights between members of different factions were quite common in Ireland at public gatherings, such as fairs and patterns, from the 17th c. until the middle of the 19th c. The most notorious factions were the Caravats and the Shanavests of Co. Kilkenny. Encounters could involve several hundred people, and the principal weapon used was a cudgel, sometimes affectionately called a kippeen; see: do be, pattern, kippeen; cf. wigs on the green.]

back, in my (getting or climbing up on my) *c. phr.* expressing dissent, implying that a statement is false, or that one is being taken advantage of. O'Casey, *J*, 87: "[H]e's goin' to pay me for that suit, or give it back - he'll not climb up my back as easily as he thinks."

back of my hand to, the *c. phr.* a deprecatory retort or refusal to shake hands. Gregory, *SP*, 92: "Let the two of you stop together, and the back of my hand to you." ["The back of my hand and the sole of my foot to you " (prov.); there are puns on the phrase in Joyce's *Finnegans Wake*: "[T]he big bag of my hamd till hem . . ." (320.08-09); "the free of my hand to him!" (308. F1).]

bad cess *excl.* bad luck. [Perh. < cess, an English military imposition on, or exaction from, the civilian population of Ireland; or aphetic (suc)cess.] Synge, *P*, 63: "[T]he thousand militia-bad cess to them –walking idle through the land." [The various kinds of cesses and their consequences are described in some detail by Edmund Spenser in *A View of the Present State of Ireland* (ca. 1596), and condemned along with other "evil customs which we have to reprove in Ireland" (81); the excl. appears in Joyce's *Finnegans Wake* as "Tuttut's cess to him!" (28.28).]

bad drop   see: drop, bad.

bad scran (scrant)   *excl.* bad luck (pej.). [< scran: rubbish, scraps of food; or perh. < Ir. *screamh*, a crust, scruff or scum.] Joyce, *FW*, 26.26-27: "Coughings all over the sanctuary, bad scrant to me aunt Florenza."

badhach (bodach, bodagh, boddah, boddagh, bodack, buddogh, buddough)   *n.* a rich lout, bumkin or clownish fellow. [< Ir. *bodach.*] Joyce, *U*, 322: "Swindled them all, skivvies and badhachs from the county Meath. . . ." Pearse, *P*, 213: "What way can we stop the bodach?" See: scivvie (skivvie).

Bagmen   see: Firbolg.

bainin   see: bawneen.

bairneach (bornack)   *n.* a limpet. [Ir. *báirneach.*] Sayers, *P*, 89: "I'd swear by the black curses that Finn put on the *báirneachs* that I'll never again touch a drop of drink. . . ." [To "swear by the black curses that Finn put on the bairneachs" is a c. phr.]

balcan   see: bulcaun.

ball of malt   *s. phr.* a glass of whiskey. O'Casey, *J*, 76: "A bottle o' stout ud be a little too heavy for me stummock afther me tay . . . . A-a-ah, I'll thry the ball o' malt." See: tay. [*A Ball of Malt and Madame Butterfly* (1973) is a collection of short stories by Benedict Kiely (1919-).]

bally   *n.* a town. [< Ir. *baile.*] Joyce, *FW*, 100.07: "Bannalanna Bangs Ballyhooly Out Of Her Buddaree Of A Bullavogue." See: banalanna, Ballyhooley, buddaree, bullavaun (bullavogue). [Bally is a com. pre. and occ. suf. in place names: e.g., Ballymun in Dublin, and Stradbally in Co. Laois, Co. Waterford and Co. Kerry (strad < Ir. *sráid*, street); Ballybeg, Co, Donegal, "a village of the mind," is the setting of a number of the plays of Brien Friel, from *Philadelphia, Here I Come!* (1964) to *Dancing at Lughnasa* (1990); "Ballyhooley" is a song by Robert Martin, brother of Violet Martin (Martin Ross of the Somerville and Ross literary partnership); "The Races of Ballyhooly" is an anti-tithe song from the period of the "tithe war" (1830-1838).]

Ballyhooly   *n.* a tongue-lashing or drubbing; after a village near Fermoy, Co. Cork, notorious for faction fights. [< Ir. *Baile átha*

hUbhla, Town of the Apple Ford.] Joyce, *FW*, 100.07: "Banna-
lanna Bangs Ballyhooly Out Of Her Buddaree Of A Bullavogue."
See: bally, banalanna, buddaree, bullavaun (bullavogue).
["Ballyhooley" is a song by Robert Martin, brother of Violet
Martin (Martin Ross of the Somerville and Ross literary partnership);
"The Races of Ballyhooly" is an anti-tithe song from the period of
the "tithe war" (1830-1838).]

bamer (baymer)   *n.* a straw hat. Joyce, *FW*, 35.13: "The latter . . .
is still berting dagabout in the same straw bamer, carryin his overgoat
under his schulder . . . ."

ban   see: bawn 1.

banacht   see: beannacht.

Banagher (Bannagher), that beats (bates, bangs)   *c. phr.* that ex-
ceedes everything; after a village in Co. Offaly. Irvine, *L*, 84: "That
bates Bannagher!" [There is a pun on the phrase in Joyce's *Finnegans
Wake*: "Mind the bank from Banagher, Mick, sir!" (87.31).]

banath   see: beannacht.

Banba (Banbha)   *n.* Ireland (lit.); after Banbha, a queen of the
Thuatha Dé Danann, pre-Celtic colonists of Ireland.] O'Casey, *S*,
10: "[M]ind you, oul' Mulligan would call himself a descendant of
the true Gaels of Banba . . . ." Corkery, *M*, 97: "[T]he myriad love-
names of Ireland were invoked . . . — The Little Dark Rose, the
Sean Bhean Bhocht, the Silk of the Kine, Innisfail, the Plain of Conn,
Fodhla, Banbha . . . ." See: Gael, Dark Rosaleen (Little Dark Rose),
poor old woman (Sean Bhean Bhocht), silk of the kine, Inisfail
(Innisfail), Plain of Conn, Fodhla. [The names of Banba's sisters,
Eire and Fodhla, are also lit. names for Ireland; "Lament for Banba"
is a poem by James Clarence Mangan; *Brian of Banba* (1904) is a
play by Bulmer Hobson (1883-1969); "Banba's Dead" and *The
Hounds of Banba* (1920) are, respectively, a poem and a collection
of short stories by Daniel Corkery.]

banbh   see: bonham.

bandjax   see: banjax.

bane   see: bawn, 1, 2.

banjax (bandjax)   *n., v.* ruin, destroy (sl., Dub.). [Perh. a comb.
of bang and axe or smash.] O'Casey, *J*, 92: "I'm tellin' you the
scholar, Bentham, made a banjax o' th' Will . . . ." O'Brien, *H*, 64.
"Some people at one time thought they were trying to banjax and
bewilder the One Holy and Apostolic."

bannacht (bannaght, bannocht)   see: beannacht.

Bannagher, that beats (bangs)   see: Banagher.

bannalanna   *n.* an ale-woman. [< Ir. *bean na leanna*.] Joyce, *FW*,
100.06: "Bannalanna Bangs Ballyhooly Out Of Her Buddaree Of A

Bullavogue." See: Ballyhooly, buddaree, bullavogue. [*Bean na Leanna* is a drinking song in Ir.]

bar *n.* a shilling (sl., Dub.): obs. since decimalization of currency in 1971; perh. from the stroke placed after a number to to indicate shillings: e.g. 10/=. Joyce, *U*, 250: "Two bar entrance, soldiers half price."

barge *v.* to scold, abuse (Uls.). [Sc.] Irvine, *L*, 139: "[W]e've barged (scolded) a lot, Anna, but we did'nt mane it."

barm brack (barmbrack, brack, barneen broec, barneenbraec) *n.* a traditional Hallowe'en currant and raisin cake. [< Ir. *bairghean breac*, speckled cake.] Joyce, *D*, 99: "These barmbracks seemed uncut; but if you went closer you would see that they had been cut into long thick even slices and were ready to be handed round at tea." [It is customary to put a wedding ring in the cake and, if a young girl gets it, she is supposed to get married the following year. The custom is the basis of the teasing of Maria in Joyce's short story "Clay" in *Dubliners* (cf. colcannon); in *Finnegans Wake* Joyce rings out the changes on the term, and towards the end of the work places its parts at opposite ends of a sentence: "Both barmhearts shall become yeastcake by their brackfest" (563.29-30).]

barnabweel (bearna baoghail) *n.* gap of danger or death. [< Ir. *beárna baoghail*, gap of danger.] O'Casey, *D*, 80: "[P]ractise . . . last stand on slopes of . . . Barnabweel. . . ." See: man in the gap. [The term is in the refrain of "A Soldier's Song," the Irish national anthem: "Tonight we man the bearna baoghail / In Erin's cause come woe or weal . . ."; it also appears in Joyce's *Finnegans Wake* as "barney brawl" (354.24); see: barney.]

barney (barny) *n.* a blunt conversation, an argument (sl., Dub.). O'Casey, *J*, 89: "I hope I'm not disturbin' you in any discussion on your forthcomin' legacy — if I may use the word — an' that you'll let me have a barny for a minute or two with you, Mr Boyle."

basthoon see: bosthoon.

baun see: bawn 1.

bauneen see: bawneen.

bawl of an ass see: ass's bawl.

bawn (baun, ban, baan, bane) 1 *a.* fair-haired, pretty, white. [< Ir. *bán*, white, fair, beloved.] Joyce, *FW*, 397.05: "And there she was right enough, that lovely sight enough, the girleen bawn asthore, as for days galore, of planxty Gregory." Colum, *PO*, 49: "My grandfather, Downall Baun, / Had a dream that comes three times . . . ." Campbell, *P*, 160: "My curse on Meehaul Ban, / The fair-haired boy, the gentleman, / That wouldn't look the road I doddered on!" See: een, asthora (asthore), planxty. [There is an obvious allusion to Augusta Gregory in the Joyce quot.; "The Bouchalleen Bawn" is a poem by John Keegan (1809-49); *The Colleen Bawn* (1860) is a very successful melodrama by Dion Boucicault, based on *The Collegians* (1829), a novel by Gerald Griffin. Boucicault's title is from a popular ballad, "Willy Reilly and the Colleen Bawn", as is the title of *Willy Reilly and His Dear Colleen Bawn* (1855), a novel by William Carleton. An operetta, *The Lily of Killarney* (1867), with words by Boucicault and John Oxenford and music by Sir Jules Benedict, is based on *The Colleen Bawn*. The plot of *The Colleen Bawn* appears in Theodore Dreiser's *American Tragedy*. "Ellen Bawn" is a poem by James Clarence Mangan; "Molly Bawn", by Samuel Lover (1797-1868), and "Nelly Bawn" are songs; "Noreen Bawn" is a song by J. M. Crofts about the perils of emigration; "The Ballad of Downal Baun" is a poem by Padraic Colum; "Childybawn" is a short story by Sean O'Faolain (b. 1900); "The Cruskeen Bawn" is a Hammersmith lounge in *Elizabeth Alone* (1973), by William Trevor (1928-　).]

bawn (baan, bane) 2　*n.* an enclosure or field near a farmhouse for cattle; occ. a deer-park. [< Ir. *ba*, cows + *dún*, a keep or fortress.] Corkery, *M*, 94: " 'Look,' and his stick swept all round the bawn fields - 'all mine, and these yonder as well - and the cattle!' " Fitzmaurice, *F*, 43: "[W]hat could be on Hanora Kennelly and everything succeeding with her? - her fine baan of cows. . . ."

bawneen (bainin, bauneen, bowneen)　*n.* a loose, off-white jacket; off-white wool or cloth. [< Ir. *báinín*.] Yeats, *PL*, 434. "He seems an Aran fisher, for he wears / The flannel bawneen . . . ." Somerville and Ross, *A*, 139: "[W]ait till I give him a couple of slaps of my bawneen, miss!" Somerville and Ross, *RM*, 112: "[M]aybe ye'll lend her the loan o' thim waders when she's rinsin yer bauneen in the river!"

bawways　*ad.* askew. Joyce, *U*, 302: "Little Alf was knocked bawways."

baymer　see: bamer.

be gorra　see: begorra.

be said by　*s. phr.* take advice from. Joyce, *D*, 194: "[S]he never would be said by me."

Bealtaine (Bealtein, Beltaine)　*n.* the month of May (lit.); an ancient Irish May-day festival. [Ir. *Bealtaine*.] Gregory, *B*. 52: "At the time [St Patrick] landed it was the feast of Bealtaine, and on that day every year the High King lighted a fire at Teamhuir, and there was geasa, that is a bond, upon the men of Ireland not to light a fire in any place before the kindling of that fire in Teamhuir." Campbell, *P*, 13: "Samhain gleans the golden harvests / Duly in their tide and time, / But my body's fruit is blasted / Barely past the Bealtein prime." Yeats, *M*, 197: "[T]hey hung the horse-thieves last Beltaine four years." See: geasa, Samhain. [During the ancient festival, a fire was kindled in the name of the god Beal (Bel), and cattle were driven between two fires as a protection against disease. *Beltaine* (1899-1900) is a theatre magazine edited by W. B. Yeats; "Antiphon: At Bealtaine" is a poem by Joseph Campbell; *Bealtaine 1916 agus Dánta Eile* (1920) is a collection of poems in Ir. by Pierce Beasley (1881-1965).]

beannacht (banacht, banath, bannacth, bannaght, bannath, bannocht) *sal.* a blessing, goodbye. [Ir. *beannacht*, a blessing.] Joyce, *D*, 196: "*Beannacht libh* [to all of you], cried Miss Ivors, with a laugh, as she ran down the staircase." ["Bannath Lath" is a poem by John K. Casey (1846-1870).]

Bearla (Beurla) English (pej.). [Ir. *Béarla*, English, poorly written Ir.] Joyce, *U*, 194: "Put beurla on it, Littlejohn."

bearna baoghal see: barnabweel.

beef to the heels (like a Mullingar heifer) *c. phr.* hefty country women; women with thick legs. Joyce, *U*, 66: "Fair day and all the beef to the heels were in." [The area around Mullingar, Co. Westmeath, is noted for fattening cattle.]

bees see: do be.

beg (beug) *a.* small, little: com, in place-names [< Ir. *beag*, small, little, minor.] Synge, *PO*, 37: "Bring Kateen-beug and Maura Jude / To dance in Beg-Innish. . . ." See: een, innis. [Ballybeg, Co, Donegal, "a village of the mind," is the setting of a number of the plays of Brien Friel, from *Philadelphia, Here I Come!* (1964) to *Dancing at Lughnasa* (1990); see: bally.]

beggar on horseback *c. phr.* applied to one who suddenly acquires power or wealth and then abuses it (pej.). Yeats, *PO*, 358: "A beggar upon horseback lashes a beggar on foot." ["Put a beggar on horseback and he'll ride to hell" (prov.); *Beggars on Horseback* (1895) is a work by E. Œ. Somerville and Martin Ross; *Put a Beggar on Horseback* (1961) is a play by Joseph McCann (1905-1980).]

begorra (be gorra, egorra, gorra) *intej.* indeed. [< by God.] Joyce, *SH*, 243. "Begorra ye'd have more trouble with the childre is in it now [than] with one of thim big fellows." [Begorra is a *sine qua non* in representations of stage-Irish speech.]

bejaysus see: Jaysus.

Beltaine see: Bealtaine.

bes see: do be.

beyant (beyont) *prep.* beyond (Uls.). [Sc. var. of beyond.] Joyce, *FW*, 215.01: "Is that the Poolbeg flasher beyant . . . ."

Ferguson, *P*, 93: "A never did insist upon / Nor ask condition beyont the one. . . ."

Bhreasail, I see: I Bhreasail.

Bianconi (bian, long car) *n.* a horse-drawn coach; after an Italian, Charles Bianconi (1785-1875), who set up an efficient network in Ireland in 1815, using long carriages drawn by four horses. Somerville and Ross, *RM*, 122: "The wing of the Bianconi had caught the wing of the smaller car, flinging Owld Bocock's mare on her side . . . ." Synge, *P*, 117: "I'd give you two kids for your dinner and a gallon of poteen, and I'd call the piper on the long car to your wedding from Crossmolina or from Ballina." See: poteen. ["In Memory of Boucicault and Bianconi" (1937) is a painting by Jack B. Yeats (1871-1957), brother of the poet, W. B.]

Biddy *n.* a plebeian woman; an obnoxious female (usu. pej.). [Abbr. of Brigid, a com. name.] Yeats, *PO*, 119: "You gave, but will not give again / Until enough of Paudeen's pence / By Biddy's halfpennys have lain / To be 'some sort of evidence,' / Before you'll put your guineas down . . . ." See: Paudeen. ["Biddy Mulligan", a popular song by Seamus Kavanagh, celebrates one of Dublin's Biddies.]

Big (Great) House, the *s.phr.* the house of an Anglo-Irish landlord; occ. a lunatic asylum (euph.). Moore, *H*, 50: "[H]e was not affected when he heard that Mary Kelly, who used to go to do the laundry at the Big House, had married . . . ." [The Big House is a recurrent theme in Anglo-Irish literature from the first A.I. novel, *Castle Rackrent* (1800) by Maria Edgeworth, to novels such as *Birchwood* (1973) and *The Book of Evidence* (1989) by John Banville (1945-), and is also prominent in the poetry of W. B. Yeats; "The Big House" is a chapter in *The Hidden Ireland* (1924) by Daniel Corkery; *The Big House* (1926) is a play by Lennox Robinson (1886-1958), a radio play (1957) by Brendan Behan and a poem by Padraic Colum; *The Big House of Inver* (1925) is a novel by E. Œ. Somerville and Martin Ross.]

big world, the *s.phr.* the world beyond the local community. [Perh. < Ir. *an domhan mór*, the big (great) world.] Synge, *R*, 13: "In the big world the old people do be leaving things after them for their sons and children, but in this place it is the young men do be leaving things behind for them that do be old." See: do be.

bird's nest *s. phr.* a Protestant institution dedicated to proselytizing (pej., Dub.). Joyce, *U*, 180: "*Bird's Nest*. . . . They say they used to give pauper children soup to change to protestants in the time of the potato blight." Cf. boiled Protestant, souper, swaddler.

bitch *n., a.* as a term of abuse, bitch can be applied to males, females and inanimate objects in H.E. Joyce, *P*, 175: "Is your lazy bitch of a brother gone out yet?"

black   *a.* extreme, bigoted; usu. applied by Catholics to Protestants. Joyce, *P*, 35: "The blackest protestant in the land would not speak the language I have heard this evening." [This usage of black is also found in Ir.: *Sasanach dubh*, a black Protestant; *an Phearsa dubh*, the black Parson. The usage may have been reinforced by the name of the Grand Black Orange Lodge of Ireland, founded in 1802, and its successor, the Imperial Grand Black Chapter of the Orange Order, members of which are known as the Blackmen.]

Black and Tans (Tans)   *nic.* an armed auxiliary force of ex-servicemen sent to Ireland by the British Government in 1920 in an attempt to suppress revolutionary activity; from the colour of their uniforms, a mixture of dark green (police) tunics and khaki (military) trousers, which reminded civilians of a well-known Co. Limerick hunt, the Scarteen Black and Tans. O'Casey, *J*, 5: "[Y]our religion is simply the state of being afraid that God will torture your soul in the next world as you are afraid the Black and Tans will torture your body in this." Joyce, *FW*, 176.24-25: "[T]he grim white and cold bet the black fighting tans . . . ." [The phrase "grim white and cold" is a pun on the colours of the rebel flag: green, white and gold (orange). The brutality of the Black and Tans greatly increased public support for independence by discrediting British rule; "Black and Tan Gun" and "The Bold Black and Tan" are nationalist ballads; *The Black and Tans* (1958) by Richard Bennett is a study of the force. The term is sometimes used for a stout and a small whiskey.]

black drop   see: drop, black.

Black Rose   see: Dark Rosaleen.

black is (was) the white of my eye (black your eye to me), say   *c. phr.* to allege any wrong-doing against the speaker. Fitzmaurice, *F*, 31: "Tut for the bishop, I'm saying, for amn't I a solid parish priest? and he dar say black your eye to me while I keep within the rules and regulations of Holy Church."

blackbird   *met.* the Young Pretender, Prince Charles Edward Stuart; a Jacobite; a rapparee; a hero (com. met. in songs). [< Ir. *londubh*, same meanings.] Ledwidge, *B*, 305: "I heard the Poor Old Woman say: / 'At break of day the fowler came, / And took my blackbirds from their songs / Who loved me well thro' shame and blame.' " See: rapparee, poor old woman; cf. wild geese. ["The Blackbirds" is a poem by Francis Ledwidge; in *An Giall* (1958), a play in Ir. by Brendan Behan, and in the early version of its English adaptation, *The Hostage* (1958), a hornpipe called "The Blackbird" is heard just before the hero, Leslie, first appears on stage at the end of

Act 1, and its title is announced at the precise moment of his appearance; "The Royal Blackbird" is a Jacobite song.]

blind nuts   *s. phr.* nuts without kernels. Somerville and Ross, *B*, 49: "It wasn't cracking blind nuts that made her that weight!"

block   *v.* fornicate (sl.). Joyce, *U*, 761: ". . . Id let him block me now flying . . . ."

bloody end to   *c. phr.* no (emph.). Joyce, *U*, 305: "Arrah! bloody end to the paw he'd paw . . . ." Joyce, *L, I*, 248: "[B]loody end to the lie in Anglo-Irish = no lie." See: arrah.

bloss   *n.* correct pronunciation of Ir. [< Ir. *blas*, taste, flavour, correct pronunciation.]   Joyce, *FW*, 479.17: "One moment now, if I foreshorten the bloss on your bleather."

blue mouldy (moulded)   *c. phr.* badly in need of something, such as a drink, for a very long time. Joyce, *U*, 298: "I was blue mouldy for the want of that pint." Somerville and Ross, *RM*, 112: ". . . I was thinkin' you were blue moulded for want of a batin' . . . ." Cf. mouldy.

blur an ages (agers)   see: tar (and ages).

bob   *n.* a shilling (sl.): obs. since decimalization of Irish currency in 1971. [Engl. sl.] O'Casey, *J*,68: "There's the five bob for yourself . . . ."

bocach (boccagh, boccah)   see: bacach.

bockedy   *a.* lame, crippled, bent, unstable, defective. [< Ir. *bacach.*] Joyce, *U*, 244: "Poor old bockedy Ben!"

bocock   see: bacach.

bodach (bodagh, boddah, boddagh, bodack, bodak)   see: badhach.

bog   *v.* to sink in a bog or soft soil. [Ir. *bog*, soft.] Somerville and Ross, *A*, 235: ". . . I have as many lies told for ye . . . as'd bog a noddy."

bog, up from the (up on the last load)   *c. phr.* a bogman, a rustic, a fool. O'Casey, *J*, 59: "[W]e're Dublin men, an' not boyos that's only afther comin' up from the bog of Allen. . . ." See: bogman. ["You can take the man out of the bog, but you can't take the bog our of the man" (prov.); *Ballads of a Bogman* is a volume by Sigerson Clifford (1913-1985).]

bog-deal (pine, oak)   *n.* wood recovered from bogs, used for a variety of purposes, from roof beams to firewood. Yeats, *M*, 226: "[T]here came in at the half door Oona, the daughter of the house, having a few bits of bog-deal from Connemara in her arms for the fire." [A splinter of bog-deal used as a torch was called a gatherie (< Ir. *geataire*); bog oak is very dark and frequently used in furniture.]

bogan (buggan)   *n.* an egg laid without a shell. [Ir. *bogán.*] Joyce,

FW, 198.26: "[S]he bogans without a band on?" *Ibid.*, 323.01: "[T]he bugganeering wanderducken . . . ."

bogman (bog-trotter)   *n.* a rustic, an uncouth person (pej., Dub.). Flanagan, *T*, 350: "They could laugh at the rest of us, call us counter-boys and bog-trotters, but they could not laugh at him." Cf. bog, up from the ["You can take the man out of the bog, but you can't take the bog out of the man" (prov.); *Ballads of a Bogman* is a volume by Sigerson Clifford (1913-1985); the term appears in A.I. literature as early as Richard Head's *Hic et Ubique* (ca. 1663).]

bohereen (bohareen, bohireen, boreen, boryeen)   *n.* a country lane, a minor road. [< Ir. *bótharín*, little road.] Pearse, *P*, 159: "Across the street with her, and down the bohereen." Somerville and Ross, *RM*, 219: "[T]he the riders followed the delusive windings of a bohireen." Yeats, *PO*, 26: "The little straws were turnin' round /Across the bare boreen." Moore, *H*, 50: "A dog howled in the distance, and the fields and the boreens between him and the dog appeared as in a crystal."

boiled Protestants   *n (pl.).* potatoes (iron.); from the practice by some Protestant of combining proselytizing with food distribution in times of famine. Joyce, *FW*, 456.03: "Tenderest bully ever I ate with the boiled protestants." Cf. bird's nest, souper, swaddler.

bollan (bullaun)   *n.* a basin-stone; a round hollow in a stone associated with a ritual site. [< Ir. *bullán*.] Campbell, *P*, 226: "A woman shows, - an empty caul - / Pouring thick cream in a bollan-stone / And quern to appease the Sidhe, who fly / Leftwise against the moon." See: shee (sidhe).

bolly   see: booley.

bona-fide (bona-feed)   *a., n.* a genuine traveller and therefore entitled to drink alcohol outside of the normal legal hours. [L. in good faith.] Synge, *P*, 67: "[W]hat would the polis want spying on me, and not a decent house within four miles, the way every living Christian is a bona fide. . . ." Somerville and Ross, *RME*, 182: "Our car pulled up at a public-house . . .; it was humming with those whom Irish publicans are pleased to call 'Bonâ feeds' . . . ." See: polis. [This legal provision was always open to abuse and was eventually abolished because it encouraged drinking and driving.]

bonham (bonamh, banbh, bonnive)   *n.* a piglet. [< Ir. *banbh.*] Cor-kery. *S*, 69: "[W]aiting up in the nights for a calf to come, or a young foal or a litter of bonamhs . . . ." Synge, *P*, 85: "[H]e'd put the fear of death into the banbhs and the screeching sows." Somer-ville and Ross, *A*, 15: "[I]t'd be no bigger than a bonnive -"

bonnyclaber   *n.* sour thick milk. [< Ir. *bainne clabair.*] Joyce, *U*, 424: "No dollop this but thick rich bonnyclaber."

book *n.* a school grade or form. Joyce, *D*, 154: ". . . Mr Power sat downstairs in the kitchen asking the children where they went to school and what book they were in."

bookil (bookul) see: bouchal.

booley (bolly) *n.* a milking place; a temporary settlement in a grassy upland to which cattle are moved in summer months. [< Ir. *buaile*.] Joyce, *FW*, 97.10: "[T]hey raced him, through Loughlinstown and Nutstown to wind him by the Boolies." [Booleying is the Irish term for transhumance; the practice is condemned by Edmund Spenser in *A View of the Present State of Ireland* (ca. 1596): "by this custom of Bollyng there grow in the meantime many great enormities unto that commonwealth" (49).]

boolumshee (bualam ski) *n.* a boaster, a talker; bomabast, nonsense. [< Ir. *bualaim sciath*, a shield-striker, a boaster.] Fitzmaurice, *F*, 15: "Isn't it me screeched the good news to Jane Quinlan, the boolumshee that will spread the good news over the known world."

boorie *n.* a shelter for cattle. [Perh. a var. of booley.] Colum, *PO*, 8: "The bond-woman comes to the boorie . . . ." See: booley.

boreen see: bohereen.

bornack see: bairneach.

bosthoon (bostoon, basthoon) *n.* a fool, a poltroon. [< Ir. *bastún*.] Beckett, *M*, 16: "[T]he incontinent bosthoons of his own class . . . were seldom at large in this shabby quarter of the city . . . ." Joyce, *D*, 160: "Is this what we pay rates for? . . . To feed and clothe these ignorant bostoons. . . ."

bothered *a.* deaf, hard of hearing. [< M. Ir. *bodar*.] Campbell, *P*, 123: "Granny Bush from her front door / Prayed the skies to rain no more. / But the gods that rule the rain / Turned a bothered ear, and fell / Straight into their dreams again . . . ." Cf. bodhaire.

bouchal (ma bouchal, avouchal, bouckil, bookil, bookul, boughal, buachall, buchel) *voc., n.* [my] boy (end.). [< Ir. *mo bhuachaill*.] Joyce, *FW*, 314.32: "[T]he youthel of his yorn shook the bouchal in his bed. . . ." *Ibid.*, 562.25: "[T]he Lord, with . . . his buchel Iosa. . . ." Fitzmaurice, *F*, 69: ". . . I can't see the bouckil himself." See: Iosa. ["Bouchaleen Dhoun" is a poem by John K. Casey (1846-1870); "The Bouchaleen Bawn" is a poem by John Keegan (1809-1849).]

bowneen see: bawneen.

bowsey (bowsy, bowsie) *n.* a ruffian (Dub.). [Perh. a var. of bousy, boozy.] O'Casey, *P*, 140: "Here, out you go, me little bowsey." Joyce, *D*, 120: "Sure, amn't I never done at the drunken bowsy ever since he left school?"

box(ing) the fox   see: nix, keep

boy Jones   *c. phr.* an informer; after Bernard Duggan, known as "the Trinity boy Jones," an associate of Robert Emmet (executed for treason, 1803), who is alleged to have been an informer. Joyce, *U*, 655. "[T]he legitimate husband happened to be a party to it owing to some anonymous letter from the usual boy Jones . . . ."

boy scout   *n.* a member of Fianna: not to be confused with a Baden-Powell Boy Scout. See: Fianna [Eireann].

Boyd's heart, break   *c. phr.* to go bankrupt or risk bankruptcy; after Walter J. Boyd, a judge in the Dublin Court of Bankruptcy from 1885 to 1897. Joyce, *U*, 626. "But even suppose it did come to planking down the needful and breaking Boyd's heart it was not so dear, purse permitting, a few guineas at the outside, considering the fare to Mullingar . . . ."

brack 1   *n.* a speck, stain, or sign of having been used. [< Ir. *breac.*] Joyce, *U*, 360: "Three and eleven she paid for those stockings in Sparrow's of George's street on the Tuesday, . . . and there wasn't a brack on them . . . ." [Tomaus Brack is an offstage character in *'Twixt the Giltinans and the Carmodys*, a play by George Fitzmaurice.]

brack 2   see: barm brack.

bracket   *a.* speckled. [< Ir. *breac.*] Gregory, *P*, 23: "Raftery a poet, and he with bracket (speckled) shins . . . ."

Brasail, Hy   see: I Bhreasail.

bray of an ass   see: ass's bawl, within an

brehon (brehon law)   *n.* a judge who administered Brehon law; the legal code which prevailed in Ireland prior to the introduction of English law. [< Ir. *breitheamh.*] Mangan, *P*, 40: "I found in the noble district of Boyle . . . Brehons. . . ." Joyce, *FW*, 59.28: "[F]olks all have it by brehemons laws. . . ." [*The Brehon Laws* (1894) is a study of the subject by Lawrence Ginnell (1854-1923); more substantial (six vols.) is *Corpus Iuris Hibernici* (1979) by Daniel A. Binchy (1900-1989).]

broken harvest   *s. phr.* a poor harvest caused by bad weather. Synge, *P*, 69: "Many [are wanting] surely, with the broken harvest and the ended wars." [The wars is an allusion to the Boer War, 1899-1902, in which Irishmen fought on both sides.]

brosna (bresna, brasna)   *n.* a bundle of sticks for fire-wood. [Ir. *brosna.*] Joyce, *FW*. 212.07: "Briery Brosna . . . ." O'Connor, *O*, 151: "Old Dan Bride was breaking brosna for the fire when he heard a step on the path. He paused, a bundle of saplings on his knee." [The Brosna river in Co. Offaly is a tributary to the Shannon.]

brothon   *n.* a thick bed-cover. [Perh. < Ir. *brothall*, warmth, comfort.] Gregory, *P*, 25: " '[H]e was hunted up from the country

of the brothons' (thick bed-coverings then made in Mayo) . . . ."
brownie *n., a.* a homosexual (sl., Dub.). Joyce, *FW*, 368.31:
"Brights, brownie eyes in bluesackin shoeings." Dunne, *G*, 176:
"[A]fter the number of times I sunk the log last night she'd never
believe I was a brownie."
buachall see: bouchal.
bucalaun *n.* ragweed. [< Ir. *buachalán*.] Yeats, *M*, 7: "The local
constable . . . advised the people to burn all the *bucalauns* (ragweed)
on the field she vanished from, because the *bucalauns* are sacred to
the faeries."
bucaugh see: bacach.
buddaree *n.* a rich, purse-proud, vulgar farmer. [< Ir. *bodaire*,
a churl.] Joyce, *FW*, 100.08: "Bannalanna Bangs Ballyhooly Out
Of Her Buddaree Of A Bullavogue." See: bannalanna, Ballyhooly,
bullavaun (bullavogue).
buggan see: bogan.
bulcaun (balcan) *n.* a strong drink; spirits made from black oats
and consumed by poorer people. [< Ir. *bolcáin*.] Hyde, *L*, 71: "Let
us roam, O my darling, afar through the mountains, / Drink milk
of the goat, wine and bulcaun in fountains . . . ." [Douglas Hyde
glosses the word: "*Cineál uisge-beatha, creidim*," (A kind of whiskey,
I believe); the word appears in A.I. literature as early as Jonathan
Swift's *Irish Eloquence* (ca. 1735).]
bullaun see: bollan.
bullavaun (bullawawn, bullavogue) *n.* a strong, rough bully.
[Perh. < Ir. *bulla*, bull + *bán*, mad, wild, or *mogh*, big.] Somerville and Ross, *RME*, 286: "[T]here wasn't a Christmas this ten
years that one hadn't a head on him the size of a bullawawn . . . ."
Joyce, *FW*, 100.08: "Banalanna Bangs Ballyhooley Out Of Her
Buddaree Of A Bullavogue." See: banalanna, Ballyhooley, buddaree.
bullawurrus *n.* a spectral bull, with fire blazing from its eyes,
nose and mouth, that guards buried treasure by night. [Perh. < Ir.
bulla, bull + *úir*, ground, the grave.] Joyce, *U*, 412. "Tare and ages,
what way would I be resting at all, he muttered thickly, and I tramping Dublin this while back with my share of songs and himself after
me the like of a soulth or a bullawurrus?" See: tare and ages, himself,
soulth. [As the syntax indicates, this quot. from Joyce's *Ulysses* is
a parody of the rendering of Irish folk speech in the works of J. M.
Synge and others.]
cabin hunting *s. phr.* going from house to house to gossip (pej.).
Sayers, *P*, 14: "[W]hen he went 'cabin hunting' in the evening he
took me with him . . . ."
caday (cadday) *n.* an idler (pej.). [Var. of Engl. caddie, one

who waits about for chance employment.] Fitzmaurice, *F*, 94: "[S]ome other smart lassie would pop up to put the come hether on softy Aeneas, leaving Eithne minus her caday of a husband. . . ." See: comether (come hether).

caed mille faltha   see: cead mille failte.

cailin   see: colleen.

cailleach (cailleac, calleac, collioch, collee)   *n.* an old woman, a hag. [Ir. *cailleach*.] Campbell, *P*, 77: "Beauty and peace I sing - / The fire on the open hearth, / The cailleach spinning at her wheel, / The plough in the broken earth." Yeats, *M*, 79: "Doubtless Clooth-na-Bare should be Cailleac Beare . . . ." Gregory, *P*, 51: "This is what the Calleac said, that was over a hundred years . . . ." ["As old as the Cailleach Beare" (c. phr.); the last sheaf in a harvest field is called the cailleach; *Hag of Beare* (1969) is a collection of poems by Michael Hartnett (1941-).]

caione   see: caoine.

cake   *n.* a round loaf of (soda) bread. Gregory, *SP*, 196: "[T]he moon was at her strength yesterday . . . and it has failed me to find on any path that cake of bread."

calleac   see: cailleach.

callogue   see: colloge.

cam (kam)   *a., n.* bent, bowed, crooked, hunch-backed; a metal vessel in which rushlights were dipped. [Ir. *cam*.] Murphy, *F*, 76:". . . Micheleen Cam! Twisted and humpy, mind and body. . . ." ["Why Thomas Cam Was Grumpy" is a poem by James Stephens (1882-1950).]

caman (camann, camun)   *n.* the curved stick used in the Gaelic game of hurley. [Ir. *camán*.] Pearse, *P*, 22: "I'd say he'd wield a camán or a pike with any boy on the mountain." Joyce, *P*, 182: "One of the Crokes made a woeful wipe at him one time with his camann . . . ." See: wipe; cf. hurley. [Because of their size and shape, camans were sometimes used instead of rifles by insurgents in training exercises or in guards of honour during the struggle for independence, and at one stage were proscribed by Br. authorities.]

can't hear one's (our, their, your) ears   *c. phr.* to be deafened or unable to hear oneself speak. Joyce, *U*, 742: "[T]he last time I was there a squad of them falling over one another and bawling you couldn't hear your ears . . . ." [The earliest recorded use of this phr. in A.I. literature is in the anon. ms. *Purgatorium Hibernicum* (ca. 1660-75).]

canavan (canavaun, cannawaun, ceanabhan, ceannbhan)   *n.* bog-cotton. [< Ir. *ceannbhán*.] Campbell, *P*, 81: "A March moon / Over the mountain crest, / *Ceanabhan* blowing; / Her neck and breast."

caoine (caione) *n., v.* lament for the dead. [< Ir. *caoineadh.*] Corkery, *S*, 82: "He played the old songs of the countryside, going straight from one to another, from a *caoine* to a reel, from a love song to a lively rattle about cattle-dealing or horse racing." Somerville and Ross, *B*, 13: "Kit had a great and grand funeral, out to the ancient graveyard on Deer Island, followed by all the country in boats and *coraghs* . . . and mourned with *caioneing* that wailed far along . . . Monarde Bay." See: curagh (coragh); cf. keen. ["Breffne Caoine" is a poem by Padraic Colum.]

Cap in hand goes through the land *prov.* humility is more effective than arrogance; from the custom of removing one's cap when addressing one's social superiors. Joyce, *U*, 167: "Cap in hand goes through the land."

Captain Moonlight see: moonlighters.

caroline *n., a* a tall hat [< L. *Carolinus*, King Charles I and II of England.] Campbell, *P*, 221: "His coat of dark-blue hammercloth, / Black satin stock and Caroline hat / Proclaim him a squire or baronet."

cashel *n.* a stone fort, a castle, a monastic settlement. [< Ir. *caiseal.*] Yeats, *M*, 86: "One day he was straying about a rath called 'Cashel Nore.' " Joyce, *FW*, 04.08: "What chance cuddleys, what cashels aired and ventilated." Colum, *PO*, 199: "The name has crumbled – Cashel that has come / From conqueror-challenging Castellum. . . ." [Cashel, Co. Tipperary, now a designated European Heritage Site, is one of the most impressive monastic settlements in Europe; *Roland Cashel* (1850) is a novel by Charles Lever (1806-1872); "Cashel of Munster" is a ballad by William English (ca. 1710- ca. 1778) and a poem by Samuel Ferguson; "At Cashel" is a poem by Padraic Colum; *The Singing Men at Cashel* (1936) is a novel by Austin Clarke (1896-1974).]

Castle Catholic *c. phr.* a Catholic who was socially and politically accepted by the British administration (pej.); a pro-British, Catholic (pej.); after Dublin Castle, nerve centre of British rule in Ireland. Behan, *H*, 157: "Get off the stage, you castle Catholic bitch." Cf. Castle hack. [Castle Catholic is one of a number of pej. terms for those who supported, or were suspected of supporting, Br. rule in Ireland. Although he does not use the term, Castle Catholics are prominent in George Moore's novel, *A Drama in Muslin* (1887), rewritten as *Muslin* (1917); the incompatibility of being a Catholic and supporter of Br. rule, which is implied by the term, is still a critical question in the North of Ireland.]

Castle hack *c. phr.* a petty informer (pej.); after Dublin Castle, nerve centre of British rule in Ireland. Joyce, *D*, 125: "They're Castle hacks . . . . I don't say Hynes . . . . No, damn it, I think he's a stroke above that . . . ." Cf. Castle Catholic, pay of the Castle, shoneen, West Briton. [Castle hack is one of a number of pej. terms for those who supported, or were suspected of supporting, Br. rule in Ireland.]

Cathleen (Kathleen, Kathaleen) ni Houlihan   *met.* Ireland: one of many code names used when patriotic references to Ireland were proscribed. Joyce, *U*, 184: "Gaptoothed Kathleen, her four beautiful green fields, the stranger in her house." O'Casey, *S*, 5: "Oh, Kathleen ni Houlihan, your way's a thorny way." See: four green fields, stranger; cf. Dark Cow, Dark Rosaleen, Granuaile, poor old woman, silk of the kine. ["Kathaleen Ny-Houlihan" is a poem by James Clarence Mangan; *The Countess Cathleen* (1892) and *Cathleen ni Houlihan* (1902) are plays by W. B. Yeats; *Kathleen Listens In* (1923) is a one-act play by Sean O'Casey; "Kathleen Mavourneen" is a popular sentimental song by Julia Crawford (ca. 1799-1860); *Kathleen Mavourneen* (1898) is a novel by Randall William MacDonnell (1870- ?); "Plan Kathleen" was the code name for a German invasion of Ireland proposed by the Irish Republican Army during the Second World War.]

caubeen   *n.* an old hat (occ. end.). [< Ir. *cáibín*.] Joyce, *U*, 192: "Stephen looked down on a wide headless caubeen, hung on his ashplanthandle over his knee." ["The Old Caubeen" is a poem by Helen Lanyon (1887-1935).]

cause, the   *n.* Irish independence. Joyce, *U*, 295. "There he is, says I, in his gloryhole, with his cruiskeen lawn and his load of papers, working for the cause." See: gloryhole, cruiskeen lawn.

cead mille failte (cead millia failtha, cead millia failtia, cead millia fealtha, caed mille faltha, kead millia failta)   *sal.* a hundred thousand welcomes: traditional Ir. and H.E. sal. [Ir. *cead míle fáilte.*] Joyce, *U*, 478: "*A streamer bearing the legends* Cead Mille Failte *and* Mah Ttob Melek Israel *spans the street.*" [Bord Failte Eireann (estd. 1955; originally called An Bord Failte) is the Irish Tourist Board.]

ceanabhan (ceannbhan)   see: canavan.

ceard (cerd)   *n.* a craftsman, an artificer, an artist (lit.). [< Ir. *ceárd.*] Campbell, *P*, 226: "A ceard / Appears, - his nature neither man's / Nor woman's, yet of both compact - / Grieving for love so stricken, art / So buried under senseless grass." Colum, *PC*, 146: "[O]ur riches were well eyed by them, / And the wrought gold which cerds of ours who have / Chief supply have customed skill in shaping. . . ."

ceoil   see: feis.

chailin   see: colleen.

chainies (chanies, chaynies)   *n (pl.).* pieces of broken china and delftware, used as play money by children. [< China.] Joyce, *P*, 35:

"[H]e had heard his father say that she was a spoiled nun and that she had come out of the convent in the Alleghanies when her brother had got the money from the savages for the trinkets and the chainies." Irvine, *L*, 55: "I'll bate ye two chanies, Hen, that I know what ye've got fur dinner th' day." See: spoiled nun; cf. chaney.

chandler   *n.* a maggot, a fly larva found in meat; com. among butchers and fishermen; perh. from the maggoty food supplied by ship chandlers.] Redmond, *S*, 6: "We fished with the larvae of the bluebottle, 'chandlers' to us, though Izaac Walton called them 'gentles' . . . ." ["Little Chandler" is the central character in Joyce's short story, "A Little Cloud", in *Dubliners*; the term appears as "chandeleure" in his *Finnegans Wake* in the context of "bouchers schurts" (64. 18-19).]

chaney (chaynee, chayney, cheney)   *n.* china and delft ware. [< China.] Fitzmaurice, *F*, 10: "[F]or its after washing up the chaney you are with the boiling water. . . ." Joyce, *FW*, 213.05: "My hands are blawcauld between isker and suda like that piece of pattern chayney there, lying below." Cf. chainies.

chapel (church)   *n.* a Catholic church: in Ireland Catholic places of worship are usu. called chapels and Protestant places of worship called churches. Joyce, *P*, 141: "A chapel, sir? Yes, sir. Church Street chapel." [A photograph of a church on the Dublin quays in the Lawrence Collection, National Library of Ireland, is labelled "ST. PAUL'S R.C. CHAPEL. DUBLIN" (1199. W.L.); the Br. Admiralty chart of Dublin Bay (No. 1415), prepared in 1874 and reprinted as recently as 1969, distinguishes between "Church" and "R.C. Chapel," but the more recent metric chart has dropped the distinction. *The Big Chapel* (1971) is a novel by Thomas Kilroy (1934-).]

chara (chairde), a   see: achora.

cheney   see: chaney.

chiernah, a   see: heirna.

child is black, the   see: Jesus Jack the child is black.

childer (childre)   *n (pl.).* children. [Rare or obs. form com. in H.E.] Joyce, *FW*, 213.30: "Wharnow are alle her childer, say?" Joyce, *SH*, 243: "Begorra ye'd have more trouble with the childre is in it now that [sic] with one of thim big fellows." See: in it. [A footnote in *Castle Rackrent* (1800) indicates that Maria Edgeworth believed the form to be obsolete: "*Childer* - this is the manner in which many of Thady's rank, and others in Ireland, *formerly* pronounced the word *children*" (18).]

chiseller (chiselur, chisler)   *n.* a boy, a child. Joyce, *U*, 94: "[T]he young chiseller suddenly got loose and over the wall with him into the Liffey." O'Casey, *J*, 58: "Chiselurs don't care a damn now about their parents . . . ." ["Chislers is Bad News" is a chapter in Tom Corkery's *Dublin* (1980).]

chitter *v.* to mutter complaints constantly. [Var. of chatter.] Joyce, *FW*, 215.31: "Can't hear with the waters of. The chittering waters of."

chree, a see: machree.

chuid, a see: achudth.

chuisle, a see: acushla.

church see: chapel.

ciarog (keeroge, keerogue) *n.* a beetle, a rogue. [Ir. *ciaróg*, a beetle.] Campbell, *P*, 91: "One *ciarog* knows another *ciarog*, / And why shouldn't I know you rogue?" Fitzmaurice, *R*, 12: "What made the case worse 'twas on the keerogue of an ash bush she landed. . . ." [*Athníonn ciaróg ciaróg eile*: One beetle (rogue) recognizes another beetle (Ir. prov.).]

ciotog see: kithog.

cipen (cipin) see: kippeen.

cish (kish) *n.* a wicker basket or pannier; also the name of a sandbank and lightship, now lighthouse, at the entrance to Dublin Bay. [< Ir. *cis*.] Joyce, *U*, 379: "[F]ar on Kish bank the anchored lightship twinkled, winked at Mr Bloom." Joyce, *FW*, 215.02: "Is that the Poolbeg flasher beyant, pharphar, or a fireboat coasting nyar the Kishtna or a glow I behold within a hedge or my Garry come back from the Indes?" See: beyant. [*A Kish of Brogues* (1899) is a collection of short stories by William Boyle (1853-1923); Kishogue (shallow kish) is a character in "The Curse of Kishogue", in *Legends and Stories of Ireland* (1831), by Samuel Lover (1797-1868); as the quots. from *Ulyssses* and *Finnegans Wake* suggest, the Kish lightship is part of the seascape of Joyce's world.]

civic guard see: garda.

clab *n.* a wide, ugly mouth (pej.). [Ir. *clab*.] Corkery, *S*, 149: ". . . . I saw his big mouth and it hanging open, dead and helpless like, you'd see the clab of an idiot."

clabber *n.* mud (Uls.). [< Ir. *clábar*.] Irvine, *L*, 116: "[D]'ye mind th' night ye come home covered wi' clabbber-" See: mind.

clash *v.* to gossip (Uls.). [Sc.] Colum, *PO*, 95: ". . . I'd let in / Oul' women who would card and spin, / And clash with me . . . ."

clashbag *n.* a gossip (Uls.). See: clash.

clawfshawn see: cnawvshawl.

cleeve (cleave) *n.* a wicker basket. [< Ir. *cliabh*.] Synge, *P*, 113: "SHAWN KEOGH *runs in carrying a cleeve on his back* . . . ."

clevy (clevvy) *n.* an open shelf or shelves in a wall. [Rare or obs. Engl.] Fitzmaurice, *F*, 22: "[H]e has such a grah for a dandy doll. . . and she sweet smiling upon the clevvy." See: agra (grah).

click *v.* to establish a potentially romantic contact with a person of the opposite sex (sl., Dub.). O'Casey, *J*, 57: "[Y]ou've clicked with someone else, me lady."

climbing up / on my back see: back, in my

cnat see: kinnat.

cnawvshawl (cnabsheal, cnamhsheal, clawfshawn) *v.* to complain, grumble or whine. [< Ir. *cnáimhseail*.] Fitzmaurice, *F*, 28: '[I]s it a gom I am to be bothering my napper with a poisoned whelp that the devil can't put a stop to ballyragging and clawfshawning from New Year's Day till New Year's Day again." See: gaum (gom), napper.

cnuceen *n.* a small hill. [< Ir. *cnoc*, hill + een, H.E. dim. suf. < Ir. *ín*.] Synge, *P*, 97: "She's above on the cnuceen, seeking the nanny goats, the way she'd have a sup of goat's milk for to colour my tea."

cod *n.* a joke, a fool. [Engl. dial.] Joyce, *P*, 43: "Some fellows had drawn it there for a cod." O'Casey, *S*, 6: "If you want to make a cod of anybody, make a cod of somebody else, an' don't be tryin' to make a cod o' me." Cf. codology. [*Godded and Codded* (1970) is a novel by Julia O'Faolain (1932-); Jack the Cod is an iron. nic. for an incompetent fisherman in *The Communication Cord* (1983), a play by Brian Friel.]

coddle *n.* a stew made from rashers, sausages, tripe, potatoes, onions and other vegetables, milk and seasonings. [Engl. since end of the 16th c.] Joyce, *FW*, 593.23. "[C]uddle up in a coddlepot . . . ." [Traditionally eaten on Saturday, coddle has been popular since the 18th c., esp. in Dublin.]

codology *n.* nonsense. [Comb. of cod + ology.] Fitzmaurice, *R*, 62: "After all what speciality could them Aygyptians have but going on with their codology." See: cod.

cog *v.* to copy; to cheat by using notes or copying the exposed work of another during an examination, or copying the homework of another. [Rare or obs. Engl. word com. in H.E.] Joyce, *FW*, 464.04: "Mark my use of you, cog! Take notice how I yemploy, crib! Be ware as you, I foil, coppy!"

cogar *v.* whisper, confide. [Ir. *cogar*.] Corkery, *H*. 15: "Cogar, . . . it wasn't any shortage of powder and ball betrayed ye?"

colcannon (kailecannon, kale-canon) *n.* a traditional (Hallowe'en) dish of potatoes mashed with butter, milk, chopped cabbage or kale and scallions. [< Ir. *cál ceannfhionn*.] Leonard, *O*, 153: "[T]he wall-eyed woman next door . . . pretended to cook colcannon . . . ." Joyce, *FW*, 456.07: "And for kailkannonkabbis gimmie Cincinnatis with Italian (*but ci vuol poco!*) ciccalick cheese, Haggis good, haggis strong, haggis never say die." Boucicault, *C*, 76: "[S]he'll get the ring itself in that helpin' of kale-canon." [It is customary at Hallowe'en to put a wedding ring in colcannon, and if a young girl gets the ring, she is supposed to marry during the following year; cf. barm brack.]

colldye *n.* a bad halfpenny; a spurious, worthless article of jewellery. Fitzmaurice, *F*, 49: "[T]he little clerks coming down from Dublin, the people praising them, but laughing in their own minds at the colldye of a thing, thinking it's Irish, they do be pronouncing through their little pusses." See: do be, puss.

collee   see: cailleach.

colleen (calleen, cailin, chailin)   *n.* a girl. [Ir. *cailín*.] O'Casey, *J*, 101: "D'jever rade 'Willie . . . Reilly . . . an' His Own . . . Colleen . . . Bawn?" Campbell, *P*, 77: "Quiet and love I sing - / The cairn on the mountain crest, / The cailin in her lover's arms, / The child at its mother's breast." See: colleen bawn. ["The Colleen Rue" is a folksong; in Ireland, unlike North America, colleen is rarely, if ever, used as a name for girls.]

colleen bawn (colleen dhas, cailin deas)   *s. phr.* a fair-haired (pretty) girl (lit.). [< Ir. *cailín bán (deas)*.] O'Casey, *J*, 101: "D'jever rade 'Willie . . . Reilly . . . an' His Own . . . Colleen . . . Bawn?" Gregory, *P*, 47: "He finds his pretty brown sister, his 'cailin deas donn,' gathering rushes in a field . . . ." See: donn. [*The Colleen Bawn* (1860) is a very successful melodrama by Dion Boucicault, based *The Collegians* (1829), a novel by Gerald Griffin. The title is from a popular ballad, "Willy Reilly and the Colleen Bawn", as is that of *Willy Reilly and His Dear Colleen Bawn* (1855), a novel by William Carleton. An operetta, *The Lily of Killarney* (1867), with words by Boucicault and John Oxenford and music by Sir Jules Benedict is based on *The Colleen Bawn*. The plot of *The Colleen Bawn* appears in Theodore Dreiser's *American Tragedy*; "Colleen Dhas Dhu" is a song.]

collioch   see: cailleach.

colloge (collogue, callogue)   *v.* to gossip, conspire or talk secretly. [Var. of colloquy.] O'Casey, *J*, 63: "D'ye mean to tell me that the pair of yous wasn't collogin' together here when me back was turned?" MacNamara, *V*, 288: ". . . I knew well there was something quare when I saw her callouging with Thomas James at the market square." See: quare.

column   see: flying column.

come-all-you (come-all-ye, cumawla)   *s. phr.* a popular song beginning with the phrase "Come all you" (occ. pej.); a long-drawn out song (pej.). Joyce, *D*, 31: "[S]treet-singers . . . sang a *come-all-you* about O'Donovan Rossa, or a ballad about the troubles in our native land." Joyce, *FW*, 399.05: "O, come all ye sweet nymphs of Dingle beach to cheer Brinabride queen from Sybil surfriding / In her curragh of shells of daughter of pearl. . . ." See: currach (curragh). [The first of eleven verses of one such song ("rude ballad", according to P. W. Joyce), "Billy Byrne of Ballymanus", is typical in theme and tone: "Come all ye brave United Men, I pray you lend an ear, / And listen to these verses I now will let you hear, / Concerning noble Billy Byrne, a man of great renown, / Who was tried and hanged at Wicklow town, a traitor to the Crown." Jeremiah O'Donovan Rossa (1831-1915) in the quot. from Joyce's *Dubliners* was a Fenian leader; his burial at Glasnevin Cemetary in Dublin, on August 1, 1915 was the occasion of a famous oration by Patrick Pearse, leader of the 1916 Rising; see: Fenian.]

comether (comedher, comedther, commedher, come hether)   *n.* a spell brought about by coaxing or making love. [Comb. of come + hither.] Joyce, *U*, 191: "She put the comether on him, sweet and twentysix." Fitzmaurice, *F*, 94: "[S]ome other smart lassie would pop up to put the come hether on softy Aeneas, leaving Eithne minus her caday of a husband. . . ." See: caday.

command   *n.* a small parcel. Somerville and Ross, *RME*, 312: " 'The commands' - i.e. some small parcels - were laid on the stone table."

conacre   *n.* the practice of subletting land in small patches for short periods at high rents, usu. to landless labourers. [Perh. < corn-acre.] Joyce, *U*, 316: "Mr Cowe Conacre: Has the right honourable gentleman's famous Mitchelstown telegram inspired the policy of gentlemen on the treasury bench?" [*Conacre* (1943) is a volume by the Uls. poet John Hewett (1907-1988).]

convey   *n., v.* the custom of accompanying an emigrant on the first stage of the journey after the American wake (farewell party). Sayers, *P*, 129: "We had a custom at that time for everyone in the parish, great and small, to 'convey' the person who was going to America." *Ibid.*, 129: "The Dunquin people had the custom in those days of 'conveying' whoever was going to America as far as the stone heap known as the Leacht."

cool   *n.* a goal, or goalkeeper, in the games of Gaelic football and hurling. [< Ir. *cúl.*] Joyce, *P*, 182: "My first cousin . . . was stripped to his buff that day minding cool for the Limericks. . . ."

coolin (cooleen, coolun, coulin)   *n.* a fair-haired girl; a celebrated Irish air; occ. hair worn in long locks. [< Ir. *cúl-fhionn*, fair-haired, or *cúilín*, the hair on the back of the head, a girl with beautiful hair.] Hyde, *L*, 71: "Whoe're saw the Cooleen in a cool dewy meadow / On a morning in summer in sunshine and shadow . . . ." Ferguson, *P*, 72: "Ah, had you seen the Coolun, / Walking down by the

Cuckoo Street, / With the dew of the meadow shining / On her milk-white twinkling feet." Hyde, *L*, 71: "There is no song in Erin more famous than the Cooleen. . . ." ["The Coolun" is a poem by Samuel Ferguson, and by James Stephens.]

coolun see: coolin.

coom *n*. a round-ended valley. [Var. of coomb, or perh. < Ir. *cúm*.] Corkery, *M*, 1: "In that round-ended valley—they call such a valley a coom—there was but one farmhouse . . . ."

coragh see: curach.

coulin see: coolin.

Cows in Connacht (faraway) have long horns *prov*. the H.E. equivalent of "Faraway hills are green," or "The grass is greener on the other side of the fence." [< Ir. *Tá adharca fada ar bhuaibh i gConnacht*.] Joyce, *U*, 328: "Cows in Connacht have long horns." [The prov. appears in A.I. literature as early as Jonathan Swift's *A Dialogue in Hibernian Style* (ca. 1735); *Faraway Cows Wear Long Horns* (1930) is a novel by William Dowsley (1871-1947).]

crack *n*. lively conversation, fun. [Perh. < Ir. *craic*, conversation, chat.] Joyce, *FW*, 221. 35: "The crack (that's Cork) from a smoker from the gods." [*Mountainy Crack* (1976) is the story of a Slieve Gullion family by Michael Murphy (1913-).]

crack, cry (cried) see: cry crack.

crawsick (cross-sick) *a*. suffering from a hangover; occ. suffering from a stomach upset. Fitzmaurice, *F*, 23: "Crawsick—a thing could happen to a man after a little booze." Joyce, *U*, 32: "You mean that knockneed mother's darling who seems to be slightly crawsick?"

crawtha *a*. angry. [< Ir. *cráidhte*, vexed, tormented, troubled, pained.] Fitzmaurice, *F*, 112: "Don't be crawtha with him, Elaine."

crawthumper (thumping . . . craw) *c. phr*. an ostentatiously devout person, a hypocrite; behaving in such a manner (pej.). Joyce, *U*, 38: "Those crawthumpers, now that's a good name for them, there's always something shiftylooking about them." O'Casey, *J*, 61: "[L]et him give his job to wan of his hymn-singin', prayer-spoutin', craw-thumpin' Confraternity men!"

creatur' (creature, craythur), the *n*. poteen or whiskey (end.). [18th c. pron. of creature com. in H.E.] Anon. song, "Tim Finnegan's Wake": "With a love of the liquor poor Tim was born, / And to help him through his work, each day, / He'd a drop of the creatur' every morn." See: poteen. [The s. phr., "a drop of the creatur', " in the song "Tim Finnegan's Wake", appears in Joyce's *Finnegans Wake* as "a drop of the cradler" (315.02).]

cree, ma see: machree.

creepie *n*. a small, three-legged stool (Uls.). [Sc.] Irvine,

L, 39: "The stools and creepies were scrubbed once a week. . . ."
cried crack see: cry crack.
crith (cruht, cruit) *n.* a hump. [< Ir. *cruit.*] Murphy, *F*, 85: "The
cruit on one, the twist to her every part. . . ." Joyce, *FW*, 549.29:
". . . I sate me and settled with the little crither of my hearth . . . ."
Cromwell (Crumwell, Crummil), the curse of *c. phr.* a com. H.E.
imprecation. Joyce, *U*, 432: "[H]e cursing the curse of Cromwell
on him, bell book and candle in Irish. . . ." [The force of this imprecation is explained in an essay by James Joyce: ". . . the great
Protector of civil rights is a savage beast who came to Ireland to
propagate his faith by fire and sword" (*CW*, 168); "The Curse of
Cromwell" is a poem by W. B. Yeats.]
croost *v.* to throw stones or clods. [< Ir. *crústa*, a clod, a missile.]
Fitzmaurice, *R*, 38: "[I]'d nearly get a fit of croosting him with
stones."
croppy *n.* a rebel, a patriot; a Catholic or nationalist (occ. pej.,
Uls.); after those of the 1798 uprising who wore close-cropped hair
as a sign of their sympathy with the French Revolution. Joyce, *U*,
31: "The black north and true blue bible. Croppies lie down." ["The
Croppy Boy" by William McBurney is the most popular ballad about
the 1798 uprising and is a motif in the "Sirens" episode of Joyce's
Ulysses, and in *How Many Miles to Babylon* (1974), a novel by Jen-
nifer Johnston (1930-); *The Croppy: A Tale of 1798* (1828) is a novel
by John Banim (1798-1842); "An old Croppy's notions . . ." is a
chapter in *Knocknagow* (1870) a novel by Charles Kickham
(1828-1882); "Croppy" is a character in "The Dane's Breechin", a
sketch in *All on the Irish Shore* (1902) by E. Œ. Somerville and Martin Ross; "Croppies lie down" in the quot. from Joyce's *Ulysses* is
an anti-Catholic Uls. slog. and a song title; "Down, Down, Croppies lie down" is a chapter in *The Orange Order* (1972) by Tony
Gray; "Requiem for the Croppies" is a poem by Seamus Heaney
(1939-).]
croppy-hole *n.* a mass grave for executed croppies. See: croppy.
cross-sick see: craw-sick.
crotal *n.* a lichen from which a red dye is made. [Ir. *crotal.*] Campbell, *P*, 42: "With the tasselled fern and crotal / Blowing softly to
the sky, / On the Golden Hills of Baile-eocain, O!"
cruach *n.* a heap, a stack, a clamp of turf. [Ir. *cruach.*] Corkery,
S, 124: "[T]he sudden downpour of rain towards the end of August
swept his newly-gathered cruach of turf from the inches, leaving him
without fuel for the coming year. . . ." See: inch.
crubeen *n.* a pig's foot, a foot (pej.); occ. a hand (pej.). [< Ir.
crúb, hoof + een, H.E. dim. suf. (< Ir. *ín*).] Yeats, *PL*, 273: "[Y]ou

took the crubeen out of the pot when nobody was looking." [Boiled pig's feet are a traditional delicacy in Ireland. At the beginning of the "Circe" episode of Joyce's *Ulyssss*, a crubeen is linked with Leopold Bloom's guilt for having abandoned his Jewish heritage; the word appears, lightly disguised, in Joyce's *Finnegans Wake*: "the ker-rybommers in their krubeems . . ." (258.35).]

cruht see: crith.

cruiskeen (cruishkeen, cruskeen, cruiskeen lawn) *n.* a little [liquor] jug; a full little [liquor] jug (end.). [< Ir. *crúiscín (lán)*.] Joyce, *U*, 295: "There he is, says I, in his gloryhole, with his cruiskeen lawn and his load of papers, working for the cause." See: gloryhole, cause. ["Cruiskeen" is the name of a headstrong mare in "A Misdeal", a story by E. OE. Somerville and Martin Ross; *Cruiskeen Lawn* is a drinking song, and notable newspaper column (1940-66) in *The Irish Times* by the novelist Flann O'Brien (Brian O'Nolan); "The Cruskeen Bawn" is a Hammersmith lounge in *Elizabeth Alone* (1973), a novel by William Trevor (1928-); see: bawn.]

cruit see: crith.

Crumwell (Crummil), the curse of see: Cromwell, the curse of

cry crack *s. phr.* to give up or surrender. Joyce, *U*, 306: "[O]ne time he led him the rounds of Dublin and . . . he never cried crack till he brought him home as drunk as a boiled owl . . . ."

cuck *n.* a small tuft of feathers on the head of a bird. [< Ir. *coc*.] Fitzmaurice, *F*, 32: "Will it keep you itself from stealing my fine young grey goose with the cuck on her head. . . ."

cuishla see: acushla.

culdee *n.* an anchorite. [< Ir. *céile Dé*, a servant of God.] Campbell, *P*, 209: "And with smooth, orient-pointed brows, / Between wax candles dimly limned, / Seven tonsured Culdees saying mass." [OEngus the Culdee (ca. 800-850) is author of *Féilire*, a calendar of saints and festivals, with a verse for every day of the year. They are the most extensive surviving collection of Old Ir. poetry.]

culligreefeens *n.* pins and needles. [< Ir. *coladh Grifín*, Griffin's sleep.] Fitzmaurice, *F*, 41: "I have cures. . . for the culligreefeens and the garradhuv . . . ." See: garradhuv.

cumann (cumman) *n.* a club, a society; a local branch of a national political party (since independence). [< Ir. *cumann*.] Joyce, *FW*, 228.12: "From prudals to the secular but from the cumman to the nowter." *Ibid.*, 320.05: "[K]erse him sagd he, . . . cummanisht sagd he, (fouyoufoukou!) . . . ." Cf. Cumann na mBan. [The blend of cumann and a H.E. pron. of communist in "cummanisht" is a typical Joycean pun. Cumann na nGaedheal is the name of a political party founded in 1923 by supporters of the Anglo-Irish Treaty (1921) which established the Irish Free State, and formed its governments until 1932.]

Cumann na mBan *n.* an association of women nationalists founded in 1913; it was, in fact if not in name, the women's auxiliary of the Irish Volunteers and, later, the Irish Republican Army. [Ir. *Cumann na mBan*, Association of Women.] Corkery, *H*, 50: "[S]he had to attend a meeting of her friends of the Cumann na mBan, to whom a young doctor was giving a series of lectures in 'First Aid.' " Cf. cumann.

cumar see: cummer.

cumawla see: come-all-you.

cumhal *n.* a female slave; a monetary unit equal in value to three milch cows. [Ir. *cumhal.*] Gregory, *B*, 47: "It was Aedh King of Ireland gave seven cumhals for his name to be given in the praising of Columcille . . . ."

cumman see: cumann.

cummer (cumar) *n.* a ravine, a valley. [< Ir. *cumar.*] Corkery, *S*, 71: 'I thought maybe music might come rising up to me out of the *cummer*, and it thronged with angels, or a great light come striking in at the window."

cupeen *n.* a shallow wooden vessel, like a soup-plate, used to bail a boat. [cup + een, H.E. dim. suf. (< Ir. *ín*).] Synge, *A*, 98: "We carried up water in the bailer—the 'cupeen' . . . ." See: een.

cúpla focal see: a chara.

curach (curachan, currach, curragh, coragh) *n.* a traditional, light rowing-boat of tarred canvas (formerly animal skin) over a wooden frame. [Ir. *curach.*] Campbell, *P*, 12: "Cliodhna's curachs, carmine-oared, / On Loch-da-linn are gleaming. . . ." *Ibid.*, 63: "The shepherd danced, the gilly ran, / The boatman left his curachan . . . ." Joyce, *FW*, 399.05: "O, come all ye sweet nymphs of Dingle beach to cheer Brinabride queen from Sybil surfriding / In her curragh of shells of daughter of pearl. . . ." Somerville and Ross, *B*, 13: "Kit had a great and grand funeral, out to the ancient graveyard on Deer Island, followed by all the country in boats and *coraghs*. . . ." See: gilly, come-all-you. [*British Corracles and Irish Currachs* (1978), by H. Hornell, is a study of the craft; *The Brendan Voyage* (1978) by Tim Severin is an account of a currach voyage from Ireland to Newfoundland in 1976-77, via Hebrides, Faroes, Iceland and Greenland, to demonstrate that such a voyage by St. Brendan (ca. 489-570), described in the *Navigatio Sancti Brandani Abbatis*, was possible.]

curate *n.* a publican's or grocer's assistant (iron.); after curate, an assistant priest to a parish priest. Joyce, *D*, 89: "He put his penny on the counter and, leaving the curate to grope for it in the gloom, retreated out of the snug as furtively as he had entered it." See: snug.

currach (curragh) see: curach.

curse of Cromwell see: Cromwell, the curse of

cushla (cushleen) see: acushla.

Dail (Doll, Doyle) [Eireann] *n.* the lower chamber of An tOireachtas, the Irish Legislature, which consists of two houses (Seanad Eireann is the upper house). [Ir. *Dáil Éireann*, Assembly of Ireland.] Macken, *SW*, 77: "[T]he new word that was emerging from the arrests and the drilling and the bonfires and the hunger strikes . . . Dáil . . . meant freedom to govern themselves." Joyce, *FW*, 322.16: "[H]aikon or hurlin, who did you do at doyle today. . . ." See: hurley (hurlin). [The two variant forms are highly unusual. *The Dáil Debate* (1971) is a play by G. P. Gallivan (1929-); *The Founding of Dáil Éireann* (1971) by Brian Farrell (1929-) is a study of the genesis of the institution; *A Fistful of Dailers* (1987) is a collection of political cartoons by Martyn Turner.]

dance Jack Latten (Lattin), I'll make you *c. phr.* a threat of severe punishment; after a Kildare man who won a wager that he would dance a distance of more than twenty miles changing his dancing-steps every furlong. Joyce, *U*, 468: "I'll make it hot for you. I'll make you dance Jack Latten for that." ["Jack Latten" is a tune.]

dander (dandther) *v.* to saunter (Uls.). [Sc. and Engl. dial.] Joyce, *U*, 614: "[T]hey dandered along past by where the empty vehicle was waiting without a fare or a jarvey." Irvine, *L*, 38: "Take a dandther down toward th' church . . . ."

Dane(s), that would perish (kill, bother, move) the *c. phr.* applied to any particularly painful physical or psychological experience; from the reputation of the Danes for toughness. Joyce, *FW*, 452.02: "[W]oabling around . . . in the coold amstophere . . . that would perish the Dane . . . ." Fitzmaurice, *F*, 5: "[T]he bitter breeze blowing from the North would perish the Danes or skin a flea itself."

Dannyman *n.* an informer; after Danny Mann, the sinister hunchback who betrays his master in *The Collegians* (1829), a novel by Gerald Griffin, and in its stage adaptation, *The Colleen Bawn* (1860), by Dion Bouciccault. Joyce, *U*, 642: "[T]here always being the offchance of a Dannyman coming forward and turning queen's evidence — or king's now . . . ." See: colleen bawn.

dark *a.* blind. [Perh. < Ir. *dall*, blind, dark.] Synge, *A*, 50: ". . . I heard a shuffling on the stairs, and the old dark man I had spoken to in the morning groped his way into the room."

Dark Cow *met.* Ireland: one of many code names used when patriotic references to Ireland were proscribed (lit.). Ledwidge, *M*, 305: "[W]hen the Dark Cow leaves the moor, / And pastures poor with greedy weeds, / Perhaps he'll hear her low at morn / Lifting her horn in pleasant meads." Cf. Cathleen (Kathleen) ni Houlihan, Dark Rosaleen, four green fields, Granuaile, poor old woman, silk of the kine. [The "Dark Cow" is a pub in "A Ball of Malt and Madame Butterfly" (1973), a short story by Benedict Kiely (1919-).]

dark foreigners   *n.* Danes (lit.). [< Ir. *Dubh-Ghall.*] Joyce, *E*, 43: "I am a descendant of the dark foreigners. . . ."

Dark Rosaleen (Roisin Dhu, Little Black Rose, Little Dark Rose)   *met.* Ireland: one of many code names used when patriotic references to Ireland were proscribed (lit.). [< Ir. *Róisín Dubh*, Little Black (Dark) Rose.] O'Casey, *S*, 7: "Now, after all me work for Dark Rosaleen, the only answer you can get from a roarin' Republican to a simple question is 'Goodby . . . ee.' "Corkery, *H*, 46: "To Roisin Dhu!" Gregory, *P*, 61: "Here are one or two of the many verses sung to the Little Black Rose by her lovers . . . ." Cf. Cathleen (Kathleen) ni Houlihan, Dark Cow, four green fields, Granuaile, poor old woman, silk of the kine. [*Róisín Dubh*, by Seán Clarárch Mac Domhnaill (1691-1754), is one of Ireland's most famous patriotic poems, translated by James Clarence Mangan as "Dark Rosaleen", by Joseph Campbell as "O Beautiful Dark Woman", and by Thomas Kinsella (1928-), as "Little Black Rose". There is an echo of Mangan's poem in Joyce's *Finnegans Wake*: "From dark Rosa Lane a sigh and a weep . . ." (93.27); *Dark Rosaleen* (1915) is a novel by M. E. Francis (ca. 1855-1930); "Róisín Dubh" is a theme in the celebrated film score of "Mise Eire" (1959) by Seán O Riada (1931-1971).]

Dark Woman   see: Dark Rosaleen.

dawney (dawny, donny)   *a.* slight, weak, in poor health. [< Ir. *donaidhe.*] O'Casey, *S*, 11: "You've said it, Mr Davoren: the son of poor oul' Batty Owens, a weeshy, dawny, bit of man that was never sober an' was always talkin' politics."

dead-man   *nic.* a life-insurance agent (iron.). Corkery, *M*, 139: "If you had an old father with a cough, or an old mother with a fatty heart, or a poor child wouldn't live to be a man—well, she'd come at the blind side of you and insure him or her . . . with a dead-man for a few pence in the week . . . and then in a year or two or three there'd be my brave Miss Nora getting her twenty, or thirty, or maybe her forty pounds from the insurance company . . . ." [At one stage it was possible to gamble thus on one's neighbours' lives, without their knowledge.]

dearg (derg, dyarrig)   *a.* red: com. in names. [Ir. *dearg.*] Joyce, *U*, 325: "[U]ttering his tribal slogan *Lamh Dearg Abu*, he drank to the undoing of his foes . . . ." ["Lamh Dearg Abu" (Red Hand of Ulster to Victory) is the slog. of the O'Neill family; "The Lough Dearg Pilgrim" (1829) and "Tubber Derg: or the Red Well" are, respectively, a sketch and a story by William Carleton; "Lawn Dyarrig" is a story by Jeremiah Curtin (1835-1906).]

deas   see: colleen bawn.

decent drop see: drop, (bad . . .)

dee *n*. pence, in pre-decimal currency (sl.); from the letter "d", the traditional symbol for pence, which appeared on the Irish farthing, halfpenny, penny, threepenny and sixpenny coins (1928-71). Beckett, *M*, 46: " 'Four dee' she said." [Replaced by the term "pee", since decimalization in 1971, from the letter "p", which appeared on all coins until the introduction of the pound coin in 1990.]

deloother (deludher, deluther) *v*. to deceive in a fawning, coaxing manner (pej.). [Perh. < Ir. *lútáil*, bowing, making up to, fawning.] Joyce, *FW*, 195.02: ". . . babbling, bubbling, chattering to herself [Anna Livia], deloothering the fields . . . ." Joyce, *U*, 447: "Humbugging and deluthering as per usual with your cock and bull story."

deoc an doruis *s. phr*. a parting drink. [< Ir. *deoch an dorais*, a drink at the door.] Joyce, *D*, 80: "Very well, then, said Ignatius Gallagher, let us have another one as a *deoc an doruis* —that's good vernacular for a small whisky I believe." [Com. in Sc. since ca. 1666 and made popular by Sir Harry Lauder (1870-1950) in the song, "A Wee Deoch an Doris".]

derg see: dearg.

deuce (juice) *n*. two pence, in pre-decimal (to 1971) currency (sl.). [Engl. for two, at dice or cards, since the early 16th c.] O'Casey, *J*, 87: "The softly I am, you know, I'd ha' lent him me last juice!" Cf. dee.

dhas (deas) see: colleen bawn (colleen dhas, cailin deas).

dhiol (dhiaoul, diaoul, dioul, diouol) *n., excl*. the devil.[< Ir. *diabhal; (tuar) m' (d') anam ón (don) diabhal*, my (your) soul from (to) the devil.] Somerville and Ross, *RM*, 275: "Howld to the stheel / Honamaundhiaoul; she'll run off like an eel!" Somerville and Ross, *RME*, 208: " *'Honomaundhiaoul! Sulluvan!'* he shouted, with a full-blown burst of ferocity . . . ." [These excls. are phonetic spellings of the Ir. excl. above.]

dhu (dhuv, du, dubh, duv) *a*. black, swarthy, dark-haired. [< Ir. *dubh*.] Joyce, *FW*, 136.30-31: "the ravens duv be pitching their dark nets . . . ." See: do be (duv be). [Donnel Dhu is the name of the prophet in *The Black Prophet* (1847), a novel by William Carleton; *Lost on Du Corrig* (1894) is a novel by Standish O'Grady (1846-1928); the "Colleen Dhas Dhu" is a song.]

dhudeen see: dudeen.

dhuv see: dhu.

diaoul see: dhiol.

diddy *n*. a woman's nipple or breast. [Perh. < Ir. *did*.] Joyce, *U*, 626: "Cuts off their diddies when they can't bear no more children."

Diehard (Die-hard, Die Hard) *n*. a militant Republican who opposed the Anglo-Irish treaty of 1921, which ended the Anglo-Irish war and established the Irish Free State. O'Casey, *J*, 100: "Ah, why didn't I remember that then he wasn't a Diehard or a Stater, but only a poor dead son!" See: Stater; cf. Irregular. [The Treaty provided a limited measure of independence and partitioned Ireland into two states, the Irish Free State and Northern Ireland. The pro and anti-Treaty forces fought a brief civil war, 1922-23, with the former emerging victorious.]

dilisk   see: dulse.

dioul (diouol)   see: dhiol.

dirty drop   see: drop.

ditch   *n*. a raised bank along a roadside or separating fields, usu. covered with a hedge; a hedge. Colum, *PO*, 13: "[Y]ou / Were out of doors and standing on the ditch. . . ." ["The best hurlers are on the ditch" (prov.).]

do be (does be, bees, bes)   *v*. the habitual present tense of the verb "to be"; it is a very prominent feature of H.E., and considered a mark of uneducated speech; bees (bes) is the Uls. and less com. form. [< Ir. *bíonn*, does be.] Joyce, *D*, 155: "I know you're a friend of his not like some of those others he does be with." Joyce, *FW*, 624.32: "Is that right what your brothermilk in Bray bes telling the district . . . ." [Does be is a *sine qua non* in representations of stage-Irish speech; there is a pun on the form in Joyce's *Finnegans Wake*: "the ravens duv be pitching their dark nets" (136.30); see: dhu (duv).]

Dolan's ass, like   see: Lanty McHale's dog.

Doll Eireann   see: Dail Eireann.

donn   *a*. brown: com. in names. [Ir. *donn*.] Colum, *PO*, 120: "One day you'll come to my husband's door, / Dermott Donn MacMorna . . . ." ["The Talking Head of Donn-Bo" is a story by Eleanor Hull (1860-1935); "An Drinaun Donn" (The Brown Blackthorn) and "Dermott Donn MacMorna" are poems by Padraic Colum.]

donny   see: dawney.

doodeen   see: dudeen.

doon (dun)   *n*. a fortress (lit.). [< Ir. *dún*.] Synge, *A*, 82: "It is a Holy Day, and I have come up to sit on the Dun while the people are at Mass." [Dun is a com. prefix in place names, such as Dun Laoghaire and Dundalk; "The Nameless Doon" is a poem by William Larminie (1850-1900).]

Doyle   see: Dail.

dreisin   see: drisheen.

dreolin   see: droleen.

drink (drop) taken   *s. phr*. intoxicated, but not totally incapacitated. Somerville and Ross, *RM*, 294: ". . . I rather feared that he was in the condition so often defined to me at Petty Sessions as 'not dhrunk but having drink taken.' " Sayers, *P*, 70: "[H]e was a real bitter boyo especially when he had a drop taken." [As the Somerville and Ross quot. suggests, in Irish courts having "drink taken" is an extenuating circumstance frequently advanced by defendants or their lawyers.]

drisheen (dreisin)   *n.* a pudding made from blood and other ingredients stuffed into the narrow intestines of sheep. [< Ir. *drisín.*] Joyce, *P*, 89: "Mr Dedalus had ordered drisheens for breakfast. . . ." Campbell, *P*, 217: "I drink / Whole draughts; imbibing, too, the smell / Of tripe, pig's knuckles and dreisin . . . ." [Drisheen is a delicacy associated with Cork; a Cork woman, with an affected accent, confuses drisheen and Dinneen (Patrick S., author of *Foclóir Gaedhilge agus Béarla: An Irish-English Dictionary,* 1927) in "Overheard in a bookshop", a section of *Hold your hour and have another* (1963), by Brendan Behan; see: hour, hold your]

droleen (dreoilin)   *n.* a wren. [< Ir. *dreoilín.*] Corkery, *S*, 198: "[M]y old friend the Dreoilin, that is, the Wren, mounted the platform and began telling us one of his innumerable stories of old time."

drop (bad, black, decent, dirty, English)   *n.* blood, ancestry. Somerville and Ross, *B*, 193: "[S]he was a . . . good big handsome healthy girl, and sensible; that was the English drop she got from her mother. . . ."

drop of the creatur' (creature, craythur), a   see: creatur'.

drop taken   see: drink taken.

dry wall   *n.* a field wall constructed without mortar. Somerville and Ross, *B*, 254: "The wall was a typical western one, built without mortar, 'a dry wall,' of large round stones, single at the top, small ones, two or three deep, at the base." [Dry walls are much more com. in the west of Ireland than in the east; they are also com. in parts of England, esp. Yorkshire.]

du   see: dhu.

Dub   *n.* a Dubliner (pej., occ. end.). Joyce, *FW*, 60.35: "The dirty dubs upin their flies. . . ."

dubh   see: dhu.

duck   *n.* a paraffin lamp. [Perh. < duck, Engl. dial., a faggot.] Corkery, *S*, 106: "At night time they set their two 'ducks' ablaze—using petrol instead of paraffin—scornful of danger . . . ."

dudeen (dudheen, dhudeen, doodeen)   *n.* a (clay) tobacco pipe with a short stem. [< Ir. *dúidín.*] Beckett, *G*, 23: "He's lost his dudeen." Joyce, *FW*, 200.18: "[D]idn't she . . . stand in her douro, puffing her old dudheen . . . ." [Daisy Crapadudeen is the iron. name of an offstage character in *The Chastitute* (1981), a play by John B. Keane.]

dulse (duileasg, dilisk)   *n.* an edible seaweed. [< Ir. *duileasc.*] Joyce, *FW*, 406.21: "Burud and dulse and typureely jam, all free of charge, aman, and." Campbell, *P*, 217: "I drink / Whole draughts; imbibing, too, the smell / Of tripe, pig's knuckles and dreisin, / Duileasg, porter, tobacco leaf . . . ." Fitzmaurice, *F*, 24: "[A] place where periwinkles are plenty, and there is dilisk thrown in heaps." See: drisheen.

dun 1   see: doon.

dun 2   *n.* end, close (lit.). [Ir. *dún.*] Campbell, *P*, 41: "She took him to Christ / (As wise women say) / Who made him a star / At dun of day."

dunch   *v.* to nudge (Uls.). [Sc.] Irvine, *L*, 58: "[T]hey 'dunched' each other and made faces."

dunder (dundther)   *v.* to knock or bang loudly (Uls.). [< Sc. dunner, to clatter.] Irvine, *L*, 84: "I dundthered at his door till he opened it. . . ."

duragh   *n.* an extra piece, a small portion given over and above what is purchased (Uls.). [< Ir. *dúthracht.*] Irvine, *L*, 43: "[A]t the close of each batch of bread I always had my 'duragh'—an extra piece of bread." Cf. tilly.

duty, Easter   *n.* the responsibility of Catholics to confess, if necessary, and receive communion at least once a year between Ash Wednesday and Trinity Sunday. Joyce, *P*, 239: "She wishes me to make my easter duty."

duv   see: dhu.

dyarrig   see: dearg.

east   *prep.* forward, up. [< Ir *soir*, east, forward, (implying motion).] Somerville and Ross, *B*, 286: "Only I seen her going east the road this good while back." Cf. west. [Traditionally in Ireland the cardinal points were designated on the assumption that one faced east; hence, *soir* (eastward, forward) and *siar* (westward, backward); the delusive meanderings of most Irish roads would make it impossible to travel for any significant distance by compass direction.]

Eblana   *n.* Dublin (lit.); after the name of the city on a map by Ptolemy, ca. 150 A.D. [Per. < Ir. *Dubh Linn*, Black Pool.] Joyce, *U*, 619: ". . . Mr Bloom gazed abstractedly for the space of half a second or so in the direction of a bucket dredger, rejoicing in the farfamed name of Eblana . . . ." [The Eblana is a Dublin theatre.]

Eblanite   *n.* a Dubliner. Joyce, *U*, 319: "The Englishman . . . came on gamey and brimful of pluck, confident of knocking out the fistic Eblanite in jigtime." See: Eblana.

eedgit, eedjiot, eedjit, eeejit, eejut, eddjit   see: ejit.

een   *dim. suf.* ubiquitous in H.E.; found, naturally, in numerous Ir. loan words, and is affixed, sometimes indiscriminately, to many Engl. words. [< Ir. dim. suf. *ín*.] O'Connor, *O*, 199: "Her speech was full of diminutives: 'childeen', 'handeen', 'boateen'." [Most words ending in een are emotive; see: shoneen (pej.), sleeveen (pej.), maneen (pej.), priesteen (pej.); and cruiskeen (end.), mavourneen (end.), houseen (end.), suppeen (end.). ["Oweneen the Sprat" is an *Irish RM* short story by E. Œ. Somerville and Martin Ross; *Don Juaneen* (1963) is a novel by John Broderick (1927-); *The Fooleen* (1968) is an early version of *A Crucial Week in the Life of a Grocer's Assistant* (1969), a play by Tom Murphy (1935-); "Thomasheen James" is a character in the short stories of Maurice Walsh (1879-1964).]

egorra   see: begorra.

Eire (Eirne, Eri)   *n.* Ireland; the official name of Ireland in the Constitution of 1937, replacing the name Irish Free State. [< *Éire*, Ireland; after Ériu a queen of the Tuatha Dé Danann pre-Celtic colonists of Ireland.] Yeats, *PO*, 51: "There was a green branch hung with many a bell / When her own people ruled this tragic Eire . . . ." Yeats, *M*, 147: "[H]is eating and sleeping places were in the five kingdoms of Eri . . . ." See: fifth. [The names of *Ériu's* sisters, *Banba* and *Fodhla*, are lit. names for Ireland.]

ejit (eedgit, eedjiot, eedjit, eeejit, eejut, eddjit, idjeet, ijit)   *n.* an idiot, fool (pej.). [H.E. pron. of idiot.] O'Casey, *B*, 447: "Don't talk like an eejut, Codger." [Ejit probably has the widest social and geographic distribution of any H.E. word.]

England's difficulty is Ireland's opportunity   *c. phr.* England's difficulty with foreign enemies, such as Spain, France and Germany, has traditionally been seen by militant Irish nationalists as an opportunity to strike for independence. Corkery, *H*, 5: "England's difficulty was Ireland's opportunity, and England had plainly never been in such difficulty." [The popularity of the phr. is probably related to its use by Theobald Wolfe Tone (1763-1798), considered to be the father of Irish Republicanism; "England's Difficulty" is a poem by Seamus Heaney (1939-).]

English pale   see: Pale, the

Eri   see: Eire.

Erin go bragh!   *slog.* Ireland for ever. [< Ir. *Éire go bráth!*] Joyce, *U*, 596: "THE CITIZEN: *Erin go bragh!*" [The slog. appears at least nine times in Joyce's *Finnegans Wake*: "For Ehren, boys, gobrawl!" (338.03); *Erin-go-Bragh*, or *Irish Life Pictures* (1859) is a work by William Hamilton Maxwell.]

eroo   see: aru.

erra (errah)   see: arrah.

fadge   *n.* a large portion of thick cake; potato bread (Uls.). [Sc.] Irvine, *L*, 43: "[S]he baked . . . 'fadge'—potato bread."

faggot   *n.* an irascible female (pej.). [Engl. dial.] Joyce, *U*, 738: "[T]hat old faggot Mrs O'Riordan that he thought he had a great leg of . . . ." See: great leg of.

faiks (faix, fegs)   *interj.* faith, indeed; usu. placed before a statement to indicate asseveration. [Var. of Engl. dial. fegs.] Fitzmaurice, *F*, 72: "[F]aix, maybe 'tis threatening you she is. . . ." Somerville and Ross, *B*, 286: "Fegs I do not." [The interj. is com. in 19th c., but rare in 20th c. texts.]

failte (failta, failtha, failtia)   see: cead mile failte.

faireen   see: fairing.

fairing (faireen)   *n.* a present, reward, or keepsake; from the practice of purchasing such tokens at fairs. Pearse, *P*, 264: "Mama will bring home a fairing to Brideen!" See: een.

fairy-cap (fairy-finger, fairy thimble)   see: luss.

faix   see: faiks.

Fal   see: Inisfail.

Famine Queen, the   *c. phr.* Queen Victoria (pej.); from her alleged indifference to the plight of the Irish during the great famine of the 1840's. O'Casey, *A, I*, 65: ". . . Victoria is known as the Great White Mother by all the people under her sway, excludin' the Fenians cruelly callin' her the Famine Queen. . . ." See: Fenian; cf. Jubilee mutton. [Records indicate that Victoria contributed £2,000 to the Famine Relief Fund early in 1847; the phr. is the title of a special number of the French journal of Maud Gonne (1866-1953).]

faral (farrel)   *n.* a griddle bread (Uls.). [Var. of fardel, a fourth part of a cake.] Irvine, *L*, 118: ". . . Mary 'wet' a pot of tea, and warmed up a few farrels of fadge. . . ." See: wet the tea, fadge.

Faraway cows   see: cows in Connacht.

farithee   see: man of the house.

farrel   see: faral.

father and mother   *s. phr.* biggest; very severe: usu. applied to something unpleasant. Joyce, *U*, 499: "Let me be going now, woman of the house, for by all the goats in Connemara I'm after having the father and mother of a bating." See: woman of the house. [As the context of the phr. indicates, it is one of a number of parodies in *Ulysses* of the rendering of Irish folk speech in the works of J. M. Synge and others.]

fealtha   see: cead mile failte.

feck   *v.* to steal; a euph. for the expl. fuck in all senses except to fornicate. Joyce, *P*, 40: "[T]hey had fecked cash out of the

rector's room." Leonard, *D*, 230: "It has feck-all to do with me."
fegs see: faiks.
feis *n.* a festival devoted to competitions in Irish song, music and
dance. [Ir. *feis*.] Joyce, *D*, 142: "Mr Bell, the second tenor, was a
fair-haired little man who competed every year for prizes at the Feis
Ceoil [Ir. of Music]."
felt *n.* a thrush. [Rare or obs. Engl.] Synge, *P*, 123: "The divil
a work, or if he did itself, . . . he'd be fooling over little birds he
had-finches and felts . . . ."
Fenian *n.* a rebel, patriot; a Catholic, a nationalist (usu. pej. Uls.);
after the Fenian movement and uprising in 1867. [< Ir. *Fianna*, a
band of warriors in Irish mythology.] Joyce, *D*, 125: "Some of these
hillsiders and fenians are a bit too clever if you ask me, said Mr Henchy." Joyce, *U*, 31: "Do you know that the orange lodges agitated
for repeal of the union twenty years before O'Connell did or before
the prelates of your communion denounced him as a demagogue?
You fenians forget some things." See: hillsiders. [Daniel O'Connell
(1775-1847), the "Liberator", Catholic leader, whose greatest achieve-
ment, Catholic Emancipation (1829), is somewhat overshadowed by
his inability to achieve the repeal of the Act of Union of Britain and
Ireland; "The Bold Fenian Men" is a popular patriotic song by
Michael Scanlan (1836-?); "The Fenians of Cahirciveen" is a song;
Fenian Fever (1971) is a book on the movement by Leon Ó Broin
(1902-).]
Fianna [Éireann] (Boy Scouts) *n.* the boy-scout movement of the
Irish Republican Army. [Ir. *Fianna Éireann*, a band of warriors in
Irish mythology.] Joyce, *P*, 202: ". . . Stephen began to quote: -
Long pace, fianna! Right incline, fianna! Fianna, by numbers, salute,
one, two!" O'Casey, *J*, 64: "He was only a chiselur of a Boy Scout
in Easter Week, when he got hit in the hip; and his arm was blew
off in the fight in O'Connell Street." See: chiseller (chiselur).
[Founded in 1909 by Countess Markievicz (1868-1927) and Bulmer
Hobson (1883-1969), Fianna Éireann prepared boys, Brendan Behan
is a notable example, for entry into the IRA. Some acted as runners
for the insurgents during the Easter Rising in 1916; *Fianna: The Voice
of Young Ireland* is the name of its magazine to which Behan contributed patriotic verse and prose. Fianna Fáil (Soldiers of Destiny)
is one of Ireland's major political parties.]
fifth *n.* a province. [<Ir *cúige*, a fifth, a province.] Corkery, *H*,
10: "[A] friend of mine . . . led the police a very pretty dance indeed, right round the Five Fifths of Eirinn . . . ." [In ancient times
Ireland had five provinces rather than the four it now has; see: four
green fields.]

figaries (figeries) *n.* elaborate decorations, notions, impulses. [Var. of fegary, a dial. form of vagary.] O'Casey, *P*, 109: "Be th' look of it, this must ha' been a general's sword . . . . All th' gold lace an' the fine figaries on it . . . ."

findrinny (findruine, findruiney) *n.* white bronze (lit.). [< Ir. *fionn-druine*.] Yeats, *PO*, 421: ". . . And wrapped in dreams rode out again / With hoofs of the pale findrinny . . . ." Campbell, *P*, 56: "Thy sons shall be as shields of findruine about thy feet. . . ." *Ibid.*, 141: "[A] crucible / Found at the foot of Cullan's hill, / And likely used by him of old / For melting findruiney and gold . . . ."

finn *a.* fair (of hair or hue), pretty. [< Ir. *fionn*.] [Finn mac-Cumhaill is the central character in the Fenian Cycle of Irish mythological tales; "Cruckhaun Finn" is a song; "Pasteen Finn" is a poem by Samuel Ferguson; the "tune" in W. B. Yeats's poem, "Two Songs Rewritten for the Tune's Sake", is the traditional "Paistin Finn"; see: pastheen (Paistin).]

Firbolg (Bagmen) *n (pl.).* mythological, pre-Celtic invaders of Ireland (occ. pej.). [< Ir. *Fir Bolga*, race of bag makers.] Joyce, *P*, 180: "[The statue of Thomas Moore] was a Firbolg in the borrowed cloak of a Milesian. . . ." Campbell, *P*, 32: "The bagmen carry the story / The circuit of Eire round, / And they sing it at fair and hurling, / From Eadair to Achill Sound." See: Eire. [Dundalk, Co. Louth, (< Ir. *Dún Dealgan*, Fort of Dalga), is named after the Firbolg chief who built the fort; the Milesians are later group of invaders.]

flahool (flahoolagh, flahoulac, flaithuil, flawhoolagh, floochalach) *a.* generous, hospitable; portly (rare). [< Ir. *flaitheamhlach*.] Joyce, *U*, 311: "[I] went in with a fellow into one of their musical evenings . . . and there was a fellow with a Ballyhooly blue ribbon badge spiffing out of him in Irish and a lot of colleen bawns going about with temperance beverages and selling medals and oranges and lemonade and a few dry old buns, gob, flahoolagh entertainment, don't be talking." Joyce, *FW*, 128.33: "[T]he flawhoolagh, the grasping one, the kindler of paschal fire. . . ." See: Ballyhooly, Colleen Bawn.

flash house *n.* a brothel (sl., Dub.). Joyce, *U*, 442: "You won't get a virgin in the flash houses."

flash lady *n.* a prostitute (sl., Dub.). Fitzmaurice, *R*, 62: "That gay fellow. . . would tell you about the flash ladies he knew that would all give out that they were parsons' daughters."

flitter (flitters) *v., n (pl.).* to scatter; shreds, tatters, small pieces. [Dial. var. of rare or obs. Engl. fitter.] O'Casey, *J*, 39: "They didn't leave a thing in the kitchen that they didn't flitter about the floor. . . ." Somerville and Ross, *A*, 84: "She. . . made flitters of herself. . . in a shop window."

floochalach see: flahool.

fluthered (floothered) *a.* drunk (sl.). Flanagan, *T*, 694: ". . . I was fluthered by God." Cf. peloothered. [The term is used by Sean O'Casey in the name of Fluther Good, a character in *The Plough and the Stars* (1926) who is "fond of his 'oil'."]

flying column (column) *n.* a small, highly-mobile, active-service unit of the Irish Republican Army during the War of Independence, 1918-21, and Civil War, 1922-23. O'Casey, *J*, 101. "If th' worst comes . . . to th' worse . . . I can join a . . . flyin' . . . column." [*Barry's Flying Column* (1971) by Ewan Butler is the story of the Cork No. 3 brigade of the IRA.]

fodeen school see: hedge school.

Fodhla *n.* Ireland (lit.); after Fódhla, a queen of the Tuatha Dé Danann, pre-Celtic colonists of Ireland.] Corkery, *M*, 97: "[T]he myriad love-names of Ireland were invoked . . . — The Little Dark Rose, the Sean Bhean Bhocht, the Silk of the Kine, Innisfail, the Plain of Conn, Fodhla, Banbha . . . ." See: Dark Rosaleen (Little Dark Rose), poor old woman (Sean Bhean Bhocht), silk of the kine, Innisfail (Innisfail), Plain of Conn, Banba. [The names of Fodhla's sisters, Eire and Banba, are also lit. names for Ireland.]

foola (foolah) *n.* a fool, a simpleton (pej.). [H.E. var. of fool.] Fitzmaurice, *F*, 52: "Foola, Jamsie Kennelly, blinded by an old vagabone's chicanery, an old toothless hag, and she surely no Linnaun Shee." Sayers, *P*, 99: "[W]hen he married a woman at all 'twasn't a foolah he married . . . ." See: lannan (linnaun) shee.

fooster (foosther, fuster, fustar) *v.* to fuss (pej.). [< Ir. *fústar*.] O'Casey, *P*, 108: "I wonder what he is foostherin' for now?" [In the "Anna Livia" episode of Joyce's *Finnegans Wake*, HCE is called "foostherfather of fingalls and dothergills" (225.14).]

foot (fut) *v.* to set sods of wet turf (peat) on end in small heaps to dry; re-futting is making the partly dried sods into larger heaps. O'Crohan, *I*, 85: "Young and old — each with his own task — footing the turf, piling it into windrows, clamping it into a rick. . . ." ["The Woman Footing Turf" is a section of *Island Cross-Talk* (1986), by Tomás O'Crohan.]

footer (futher) *v.* to bumble (pej.). [< Ir. *fútar*.] Joyce, *FW*, 556.24: "The infant Isabella from her coign to do obeisance towards the dufgerent, as furst futherer with drawn brand." [There is a pun in this quot. on "first footer", the first person met, or to visit one's home, on New Year's Day; it is an unlucky sign if the person has red hair (folk.).]

foreby *prep., adv.* besides, as well as (Uls.). [Comb. of for + by: rare or obs. Engl.] Irvine, *L*, 48: "[E]verybody would know that ye didn't grow it — forby they know that th' smoke in here would kill it in a few days."

forenenst (foreninst, fornent, forenint, forenist, forninst) *prep.*, *adv.* opposite, in front of, against. [Comb. of fore + anent: rare or obs. Engl.] Joyce, *FW*, 626.15: "One time you'd stand forenenst me, fairly laughing, in your bark and tan billows of branches for to fan me coolly." *Ibid.*, 21.16: "And the prankquean pulled a rosy one and made her wit foreninst the dour." See: black and tan (bark and tan), rossy (rosy), one.

forgetful people see: gentle folk.

four bones *s. phr.* body. Joyce, *U*, 212: "[I]t is petrified on his tombstone under which her four bones are not to be laid."

four green fields (lost green fields) *met.* Ireland, the four provinces of Ireland (Leinster, Munster, Connacht, and Ulster); one of many code terms for Ireland when patriotic references to the country were proscribed; since Independence, Uls. has been called the "lost green field," because it remains under Br. rule. Joyce, *U*, 184: "Gaptoothed Kathleen, her four beautiful green fields, the stranger in her house." See: fifth, Cathleen ni Houlihan (Kathleen), stranger; cf. Dark Cow, Dark Rosaleen, Granuaile, poor old woman, silk of the kine. [Stephen Dedalus, in the quot.from *Ulysses*, echoes the Old Woman in Yeats's *Cathleen ni Houlihan* (1902): "My four beautiful green fields" (*PL*, 81); "Four Green Fields" is a song by the folksinger Tommy Makem.]

fraughans (fraughauns, fraochans, fraycawns) *n (pl.).* whortleberries. [Ir. *fraochán*.] Fitzmaurice, *R*, 12: "It's picking fraycawns Mary was." ["Fraocháns" is a poem by Joseph Campbell.]

Free Stater see: Stater.

freet *n.* a superstition, a superstitious rite (Uls.). [Sc.] Joyce, *FW*, 11.06: "Her would be too moochy afreet."

fret *n.* doom. [Obs. or rare Engl.] Yeats, *M*, 14: " 'The fret' (Irish for doom) 'is over me,' he repeated, and then went on to talk once more of God and Heaven."

frighteous (frightus) *n.* paralysis caused by an attack of nerves. Joyce, *FW*, 343.34-35: ". . . I no sooner seen aghist of his frighteousness then I was bibbering with vear . . . ."

frish-frash *n.* a gruel made from Indian meal (corn) and other ingredients. Synge, *P*, 2, 107: "[T]hey'd put him in a narrow grave, with cheap sacking wrapping him round, and pour down quicklime on his head, the way you'd see a woman pouring any frish-frash from a cup."

fuillilaloo see: alilu.

full of a door (dure), the *s. phr.* a big person. Joyce, *U*, 425: "Know his dona? Yup, sartin, I do. Full of a dure."

fuster (fustar)   see: fooster.

fut   see: foot.

futhering   see: footering.

g.p.   *n.* a glass (half pint) of plain (porter). Joyce, *D*, 88: "Here, Pat, give us a g.p., like a good fellow." See: glass.

gabhail   see: gwal.

gad   *n.* a withe, a flexible twig suitable for binding things together. [Ir. *gad.*] Gregory, *SP*, 190: "What is there but love can twist a man's life, as easily as sally rods are twisted for a gad?"

Gael (Gaedhal)   *n.* the Irish, particularly the Celtic Irish, as distinct from the English and other post-Celtic invaders of Ireland. [< Ir. *Gaedheal.*] Yeats and Gregory, *U*, 153: "It is he would have got leave for the Gael to be as high as the Gall." Campbell, *P*, 11: "The strong shall go down, / And the weak shall prevail, / And a glory shall sit / On the sign of the Gaedhal." See: Gall. ["The Captivity of the Gaels" is a poem by James Clarence Mangan; "The Downfall of the Gael" is a poem by Samuel Ferguson; *Bards of the Gael and Gall* (1897) is an influential anthology of poems by George Sigerson (1836-1925); *The Gael* is the weekly newspaper published by the Gaelic Athletic Association and later a monthly magazine published in New York both of which featured the writers of the Irish Literary Revival; "Peace and the Gael" (1915) is a brief essay on the coming revolution in Ireland by Patrick Pearse, leader of the Easter Rising of 1916; *The Gael* (1919) is a novel by Edward E. Lysaght.]

Gaeltacht (Gaedhaldacht)   *n.* an area in which Ir. (Gaelic) is the vernacular; Gaeldom. [Ir. *Gaedhealtacht.*] Behan, *W*, 140: "[I]t wasn't the declining Gaeltacht was knotting his brow nor the lost green field. . . ." Campbell, *P*, 11: "Strange words I heard said / At the fair of Dún-eas — / 'The Gaedhaldacht shall live, The Galldacht shall pass!' " See: four green fields (lost green field), doon (Dún), Galldacht. [In the "Gaeltacht Areas Order" (1956) Gaeltacht areas were declared in the counties of Clare, Cork, Donegal, Galway, Kerry, Mayo and Waterford.]

gaffer   *n.* a boy, a young man. [< Engl. gaffer, a foreman, an elderly person entitled to respect.] Synge, *P*, 173: "Ten thousand blessings upon all that's here, for you've turned me a likely gaffer in the end of all . . . ."

gag   *n.* a conceited or foppish young man. Joyce, *FW*, 516.03: ". . . Meesta Cheeryman, first he come up, a gag as a gig. . . ."

gale day   *n.* the twice-yearly day, usu. the first of May and November, on which rents were paid by tenants to landlords. [< gavel.] Moore, *M*, 102: "They had for certainly three generations lived in comfortable idleness, watching from their big square houses the different collections of hamlets toiling and moiling, and paying their rents every gale day." [A hanging-gale was an arrears of rent; *Gale Day* (1979) is a play by Eugene McCabe.]

Gall   *n.* foreigners, particularly the English, but applied in succession to the various post-Celtic invaders of Ireland (lit.). [< Ir. *Gall.*] Yeats and Gregory, *U*, 153: "It is he would have got leave for the Gael to be as high as the Gall." See: Gael; cf. stranger. [*Bards of the Gael and Gall* (1897) is an influential anthology of poems by George Sigerson (1836-1925); Diarmuid MacMurrough (1110-1171), king of Leinster, who invited the Normans to Ireland, is known as Diarmuid na nGall.]

Galldacht   *n.* English influence; an English-speaking district. [Ir. *Galldacht.*] Campbell, *P*, 11: "Strange words I heard said / At the fair of Dún-ease — / 'The Gaedhaldacht shall live, The Galldacht shall pass!' " See: doon (Dún); cf. Gaeltacht.

galloglass   *n.* a heavily armed, Scottish mercenary soldier, 13th to 16th c., who fought with the N. Irish against the Normans and English. [< Ir. *gallóglach*, foreign soldier.] Corkery, *H*, 11: "Their forefathers had been doing as much for the hunted Gaels of four centuries — those shadowy, unnamed warriors, poets, stragglers, kernes, galloglasses, tories, rapparees, outlaws, whiteboys, fenians . . . ." See: Gael, kerne, tory, rapparee, whiteboy, Fenian. [Gallowglass is one of the identities of the narrator of "The More A Man Has The More A Man Wants", a poem by Paul Muldoon (1951-).]

gallous (gallus)   *a.* fine. [Var. of gallows.] Synge, *P*, 153: "Father Reilly's after reading it in gallous Latin." Joyce, *U*, 199:" 'Twas murmur we did it for a gallus potion would rouse a friar, I'm thinking, and he limp with leching." [The quot. from Joyce's *Ulysses* is one of a number of parodies in the work of the rendering of Irish folkspeech by J. M. Synge and others.]

galluses (gallowses)   *n.* suspenders. [(Double) pl. of gallows.] Somerville and Ross, *RM*, 264: "[I]n the course of the first lap what were described as 'his galluses' abruptly severed their connection with the garments for whose safety they were responsible. . . ." Pearse, *P*, 158: "She minded then that she had neither belt nor gallowses." See: mind (minded).

game ball   *c. phr.* good or excellent. Joyce, *P*, 105: "A tall boy behind Stephen rubbed his hands and said: — That's game ball."

gap of danger (death)   see: man in the gap.

garda (garda siochana, guard, civic guard)   *n.* a policeman (since

Independence). [< Ir. *Garda Síochána,* Civic Guard.] Joyce, *FW,* 197.07: "Ask Lictor Hackett or Lector Reade of Garda Growley or the Boy with the Billyclub." O'Casey, *J,* 82: ". . . I'd call you a real thrue Diehard an' live-soft Republican, attendin' Republican funerals in the day, an' stoppin up half the night makin' suits for the Civic Guards!" See: Diehard; cf. peeler (Royal Irish Constabulary). [The Civic Guard, an unarmed force, was established to replace the paramilitary Royal Irish Constabulary by an act of the Irish Free State on August 8, 1923; the Garda Siochana Act of 1958 provided for the entry of women, banghardai, into the force. *Letters of a Civic Guard* (1976) is an epistolary novella by John B. Keane; a civic guard barracks is the setting of *The Barracks* (1963) by John McGahern (1935-).]

gardai (guards, civic guards)   *n (pl.).* police. [Ir. *gárdaí.*] See: garda.

garradhuv   *n.* an intestinal disorder. [Perh. < Ir. *garr,* ordure in the intestines + *dubh,* black.] Fitzmaurice, *F,* 55: "Cures I have for the culligreefeens and cures galore for the garradhuv. . . ." See: culligreefeens.

garran (garron, garraun)   *n.* an old horse, a nag. [< Ir. *gearrán.*] Yeats, *M,* 196: "[T]he horseman was near enough for . . . the rough-haired garron under him, to be seen . . . ." [The word appears in A.I. literature as early as *A Dialogue in Hibernian Style* (ca. 1735) by Jonathan Swift (1667-1745); "The Garraun Bwee" is an air; Knockgarrons is a castle in *The O'Briens and the O'Flahertys* (1827) by Lady Morgan (ca. 1776-1859); there is a Garron Point on the Co. Antrim coast.]

Garret Reilly   see: whole world and Garret Reilly, the

garsoon   see: gorsoon.

gas   *n.* fun (sl.). Joyce, *D,* 22: "[H]e told me he had brought it to have some gas with the birds." [There is a pun on the term in the title of Joyce's verse broadside, "Gas from a Burner" (1912).]

gash   *n.* an ornamental, curved flourish made with a pen at the end of a piece of writing. Joyce, *FW,* 124.02: "The original document . . . showed no signs of punctuation of any sort. Yet . . . it was pierced butnot punctured . . . by numerous stabs and foliated gashes made with by a pronged instrument. These paper wounds . . . were gradually and correctly understood to mean stop . . . ."

gassoon (gassan)   see: gorsoon.

gatch   *n.* an affected gesture or movement; a swagger or distinctive gait (Cork). Joyce, *FW,* 288.F7: "Has our retrospectable fearfurther gatch mutchtatches?"

gatherie   see: bogdeal.

gaum (gawm, gom, gommagh, gommoch, gomeral, gomeril) *n.* a soft, foolish person; a fool (pej.). [Perh. < Ir. *gamal* or *gomach*, or Engl. gomerel.] O'Casey, *C*, 386: "That's not where th' evil is, the gaum, if he want's to know." Somerville and Ross, *RME*, 318: " 'What ails ye,' says I, 'ye old gommoch, that ye'd let the dog kill me chickens?' " Irvine, *L*, 80: "I was fixin' m' galluses over Crawford's hedge, whin some gomeral luked over an' says, says he: 'Morra, Hughie!' " See: galluses, Gomorrah (Morra).

gazebo (gesabo, gazaybo) *n.* a tall or elaborate structure or contraption (usu. pej.); a tall, awkward or foolish person (pej.); from gazebo, a raised turret on top of a house or a garden house commanding a fine view (such structures were frequently incongruous). Yeats, *PO*, 264: "We the great gazebo built, / They convicted us of guilt . . . ." Joyce, *U*, 779: ". . . Im sure Im not going to take in lodgers off the street for him if he takes a gesabo of a house like this . . . ." Fitzmaurice, *F*, 26: "[I]n a manner we're in three gazaybos that were feared, respected and venerated men." ["Gazebos and Gashouses" is a chapter in *Eminent Domain* (1967) by Richard Ellmann (1918-1988); see: gas.]

geasa (gease) *n.* a taboo, a bond (lit.). [< Ir. *geas*.] Gregory, *B*. 52: "[T]here was geasa, that is a bond, upon the men of Ireland not to light a fire in any place before the kindling of that fire in Teamhuir." Fitzmaurice, *F*, 79: " 'Twas long enough . . . for old King Brian to be putting you under gease because of your courting his son. . . ." See: Bealtaine. [In Yeats's poem "Cuchulain's Fight with the Sea", and the story in *Táin Bó Cuailnge*, the chief saga of the Ulster Cycle of Irish mythology on which the poem is based, Cuchulain is tricked into killing his son because of such a taboo. Geashill is a village in Co. Offaly.]

gee *n.* vulva, vagina (sl., Dub.). Joyce, *FW*, 112.06: "Gee up, girly!" Doyle, *V*, 65: "[H]e'd had to keep feeling them up and down from her knees up to her gee. . . ." [The term appears at least twelve times in Joyce's *Finnegans Wake*.]

gent (gentleman) who pays the rent (rate) *c. phr.* a pig; selling the family pig was, at one time, the only source of cash for many tenant farmers. Joyce, *FW*, 86.27: "[T]he pikey later selling the gentleman ratepayer . . . in order to pay off . . . fifteen arrears of his, the villain's not the rumbler's rent." *Ibid.*, 89.15: "Bejacob's, just a gent who prayed his lent."

gentle *a., euph.* applied to a place or thing associated with the fairies. See: gentle folk.

gentle folk (good folk, wee folk, good people, little people, forgetful people) *s. phr., euph.* the fairies. [< Ir. *na daoine maithe*, the good people; *na daoine beaga*, the little people.] Yeats, *M*, 55: "She next saw . . . a quantity of little people." *Ibid.*, 54: "We talked of the Forgetful People, as the faery people are sometimes called . . . ." Cf. away, them. [These euphs. are a manifestation of a universal reluctance to name things that are feared.]

George   see: Shane Bwee.

gesabo   see: gazebo.

get (gett)   *n.* a bastard (pej.). [< beget.] Joyce, *U*, 325: "The curse of a goodfornothing God light sideways on the bloody thicklugged sons of whores' gets!" O'Casey, *C*, 387: "You one-eyed gett, if you had two, I'd cyclonise you with a box!"

get . . . death   *v.* to die. [< Ir. *bás d'fagháil*.] Joyce, *D*, 221: "I implored him to go home at once and told him he would get his death in the rain." [This idiom provides a good illustration of the influence of Ir. on H.E.: in Ir., one does not die, one "gets death" (*bás d'fagháil*).]

getting up on my back   see: back, in my

gey   *adv.* very (Uls.). [Sc. var. of gay.] Irvine, *L*, 18: "Some said she would make 'a gey good schoolmistress', for she was fond of children."

ghosther   see: goster.

gilly   *n.* a servant. [< Ir. *giolla*.] Campbell, *P*, 61: "I am the gilly of Christ, / The mate of Mary's Son; / I run the roads at seeding-time, / And when the harvest's done." ["The Adventures of Gilla na Chreck" is a story by Patrick Kennedy (1801-1873); *The Gilly of Christ* (1907) is a volume of poems by Joseph Campbell; "Gilly" is a story by Edna O'Brien (1932-).]

Ginny Joe   see: jinnyjo.

gipo (gypo)   *n.* semen (sl., Dub.). Joyce, *FW*, 276.17: "Gippo, good oil!" [Gypo Nolan is the central character in *The Informer* (1925) a novel by Liam O'Flaherty (1896-1984).]

girsha   *n.* a little girl (end.). [< Ir. *girseach*.] Colum, *PO*, 64: "He sings to the *girsha* in the hazle-wood cover."

glamour   *v., n.* a spell cast on humans by fairies. [Sc.] Yeats, *M*, 72: "[H]is mother was glamoured by the fairies and imprisoned for the time in a house in Glasgow . . . ." *Ibid.*, 73: "[S]he was trying to cast on him the glamour by giving him faery food, that she might keep him with her . . . ." Cf. glaum. [The word was introduced to the literary language by Sir Walter Scott (1771-1832).]

glass   *n.* a half pint (of beer). Joyce, *D*, 89: "The curate brought him a glass of plain porter." See: curate. ["A Glass of Beer" is a poem by James Stephens; Christy Mahon's first action in *The Playboy of the Western World*, by J. M. Synge, is to order a glass of porter. In Irish pubs beer is ordered by the glass, not the half pint.]

glaum (glawm) *n., v.* grasp, maul or pull about with the hands. [< Ir. *glám*, grasp.] Joyce, *FW*, 600.36: "[T]hat look whose glaum is sure he means bisnisgels to empalmover." Joyce, *U*, 743: "[S]he used to be always embracing me Jose whenever he was there meaning him of course glauming me over. . . ." Corkery, *S*, 52: "[H]e began to glawm his breast . . . ." Cf. glamour.

glib (glibb) *n.* hair worn in a thick, matted mass on the forehead and over the eyes; a former Irish custom proscribed by various English statutes. [< Ir. *glib*.] Campbell, *P*, 215: "But, most, / Trooped in the country folk: poor kerns, / Wild in shag rugs (so Derrek's pen / Drew them), with glibbs of matted hair . . . ." [In his *View of the Present State of Ireland* (ca. 1596), Edmund Spenser took particular exception to the custom: ". . . Irish glibs . . . besides their savage brutishness and loathly filthiness, which is not to be named, they are fit masks as a mantle is for a thief, for whensoever he hath run himself into that peril of law that he will not be known, he either cutteth off his glibb quite, by which he becometh nothing like himself, or pulleth it so low down over his eyes that it is very hard to discern his thievish countenance . . ." (53).]

gloryhole *n.* a storage place, usu. under stairs, where all sorts of odds and ends are stored or dumped (iron.). Joyce, *U*, 295: "There he is, says I, in his gloryhole, with his cruiskeen lawn and his load of papers, working for the cause." See: cruiskeen, cause.

glugger *n.* an addled egg, or one that does not hatch; empty noise; a foolish boaster. [< Ir. *gliogar*.] Fitzmaurice, *F*, 103: "[Y]ou guessed there would be one glugger in the clutch of eggs you got from Mrs Dempsy." [Glugg or Glugger is a character in Joyce's *Finnegans Wake* (240.03).]

go-by-the-wall (and tickle-the-bricks) *c. phr.* a sly, sneaky person, a hypocrite. Joyce, *P*, 201: "Did you ever see such a go-by-the-wall?"

gob *n.* mouth (pej.). [< Ir. *gob*, a beak-like mouth.] Synge, *P*, 119: "An ugly young streeler with a murderous gob on him and a little switch in his hand." See: streel.

goleen see: gwal.

gom see: gaum.

gombeen (man) *n.* an individual, usu. a huxter, who engages in usury; more recently applied to a small-town or rural entrepreneur involved in a number of enterprises, and to the type of political and economic opportunist who emeged following Irish independence (pej.). [< Ir. *gaimbín*, usury.] Campbell *P*, 117: "Behind a web of bottles, bales, / Tobacco, sugar, coffin nails / The gombeen like a spider sits, / Surfeited; and for all his wits, / As meagre as the

tally-board / On which his usuries are scored." Cf. gombeenery.
[Gombeen men were sometimes called "meal-mongers", as in *The
Black Prophet* (1847) by William Carleton, and their interest rates
were as high as 600% per annum; "The Gombeen" is a poem by
Joseph Campbell; *The Gombeen Man* (1913) is a play by R. J. Ray
(1865- ?); *Gombeen* (1985) is a play by Seamus Finnegan (1949-).]
gombeenery (gombeenism)   *n.* the political, economic and social
control of communities by gombeen men. MacNamara, *V*, 49: "[I]t
was here she must buy her few groceries, for this was the principal
house of Garradrimna and, even so far as her, the octopus of Gombeenism was sure to extend itself." See: gombeen.
gomeral (gomeril)   see: gaum.
gommoch   see: gaum.
Gomorrah (Morra, Morrow)   *sal.* Good morrow. [H.E. pron. and
abbr. of rare or obs. Engl. sal. com. in H.E.] Joyce, *FW*, 579.23:
"Gomorrha. Salong." Irvine, *L*, 80: "I was fixing' m' galluses over
Crawford's hedge, whin some gomeral luked over an' says, says he:
'Morra, Hughie!' " See: galluses, gaum (gomeral). [The context of
the Joyce quot. indicates a pun on the name of the Biblical city.]
good folk (people)   see: gentle folk.
good warrant   see: warrant.
goody   *n.* a dish of bread and sugar mashed in warm milk for
infants and invalids. [< goody, a sweetmeat.] Joyce, *FW*, 256.18:
"Too soon are coming tasbooks and goody, hominy bread and
bible bee. . . ."
gorb   *n.* a ravenous eater, a glutton (Uls.). [Ir. *gorb*.] Joyce, *FW*,
31.12: "Our sailor king, who was draining a gugglet of obvious
adamale, gift both and gorban, upon this, ceasing to swallow, smil-
ed most heartily . . . ." ["Adam's ale," a jocular term for water,
appears to be conflated with "a damn male" in "adamale."]
gorra   see: begorra.
gorsoon (gosoon, gosson, gossoon, garsoon, gassoon, gassan)   *n.*
a boy. [< Ir. *garsún*, < Fr. *garçon*.] Joyce, *FW*, 377.25: "[T]hrowing
lots inside to know whose to be their gosson. . . ." Joyce, *U*, 43:
"I was a strapping young gossoon at that time . . . ." Fitzmaurice,
F, 26: "I'm only as you might say the garsoon, the messenger from
James and old Mohoon." [*The New Gossoon* (1930) is a play by
George Shiels (1881-1949).]
goster (gosther, ghosther)   *n., v.* gossipy conversation. [Perh. <
Ir. *gasrán*, a conversation.] Joyce, *D*, 127: "[H]e was leaning on
the counter in his shirt-sleeves having a deep goster with Alderman
Cowley." O'Casey, *S*, 8: "I've no time to be standin' here gostherin'
with you . . . ."

gouger (gougher, gowger) *n.* a cheat, ruffian (sl., Dub.). O'Casey, *S*, 33: "[Y]ou're a man, an' not like some of the goughers in this house, that ud hang you."

gowl *v.* to growl; occ. to cry or whinge (Uls.). [Sc.] Irvine, *L*, 136: "I hate a maan that gowls . . . ."

gra (grah) see: agra.

grabber *n.* an individual who took over the land of an evicted tenant farmer, particularly during the period of the Land War, 1879-1903 (pej.). MacNamara, *V*, 126: "The word 'grabber' had not been invented to describe a new class, but rather to denote the remarkable character of a class already in existence."

gradh (geal), a see: agra.

gradhbhar see: grauver.

gragh (grah) see: agra.

grainne oge *n.* a hedgehog. [Ir. *Gráinneog.*] Yeats, *M*, 60: "He has heard the hedgehog — 'grainne oge,' he calls him — 'grunting like a Christian. . . ." See: Og (oge).

gramachree see: agra and machree.

Granuaile (Grania Waile, Graunia, Granuweal) *met.* Ireland: one of many code names used when patriotic reference to Ireland were proscribed (lit.); after *Gráinne Uí Mháille* (Grace O'Malley, ca. 1530-1603), a colourful leader and sea captain, pirate according to some accounts, in Mayo and along the west coast of Ireland. Gregory, *SP*, 25: "As she sang her song it was on the wrong of poor old Granuaile." Cf. Cathleen (Kathleen) ni Houlihan, Dark Cow, Dark Rosaleen (Woman), four green fields, poor old woman, silk of the kine. [In Joyce's *Finnegans Wake*, "grannewwail" (22.12) is an important figure. The story of her alleged kidnapping of the son of the Earl of Howth is woven into the tale of Jarl van Hoother and the Prankquean: "her grace o' malice kidsnapped up the jiminy Tristopher" (21.20-21); her ferocity is suggested in some of the puns on her name: "grace a mauling" (115.20); "grace so madlley "(335.31). "Granuaile", "Poor Old Granuaile" and "Granuweal" are songs; "Grace O'Malley" is a poem by Samuel Ferguson; *Grania* (1892) is a romantic tale by Emily Lawless (1845-1913); *The Pirate Queen of Connacht* (1980), by Shaun Herron (1912-), and *Mistress of the Eagles* (1990), by the Canadian writer Elona Malterre, are novels based on the life of Granuaile; *Granuaile* (1979) by Anne Chambers (1950-) is a biography; "Granuaile" is one of the ships of the Irish lighthouse service.]

grauver (gradhbhar) *a.* affable, generous, affectionate. [< Ir. *grádhmhar.*] Somerville and Ross, *RME*, 200 "[T]hey told me . . . that I was a fine *grauver* of a man, and it was a pity there weren't more like me . . . ."

graw   see: agra.

Great House   see: Big House.

great leg of (leg of)   *s. phr.* having considerable influence on, or standing with. Joyce, *U*, 738: "[T]hat old faggot Mrs O'Riordan that he thought he had a great leg of . . . ." See: faggot.

great warrant   see: warrant.

great wish (wish)   *s. phr., n.* great esteem; respect [< Ir. *meas mór.*] Joyce. *D*, 10: "The old chap taught him a great deal, mind you; and they say he had a great wish for him." Gregory, *P*, 39: "[T]he people from the village followed him, for they all had a wish for Raftery." [This expression, like its Ir. source, has no sexual connotations.]

great with   *s. phr.* very friendly with. [< Ir. *mór le.*] Joyce, *D*, 220: "I was great with him at that time, she said." [This phrase, like its Ir. source, usu. has no sexual connotations.]

green fields, four (lost green field)   see: four green fields.

greenhouse   *n.* one of the hexagonal, cast-iron, public urinals, which used to be part of Dublin's street furniture (sl.); from the colour they were painted. Joyce, *U*, 153: "That quack doctor for the clap used to be stuck up in all the greenhouses."

grianaun   *n.* a sunny chamber or balcony; a summer-house. [< Ir. *grianán.*] Joyce, *U*, 332: "The scenes . . . showing our ancient duns and raths and cromlechs and grianauns. . . ." See: doon (dun).

grig (greg)   *v.* to tantalize. [< Ir. *griog.*] Joyce, *FW*, 139.18: "Ann alive, the lisp of her, 'twould grig mountains . . . ."

gripe (grype)   *n.* a trench, usu. beside a high ditch or fence. [Engl. dial.] Synge, *P*, 65: ". . . I've heard tell there's a queer fellow above going mad or getting his death, maybe in the gripe of the ditch. . . ." Sayers, *P*, 108: "He gave a wild jump from the top of the fence and got his footing on a green tuft of grass growing on the other side of the grype." See: get. . .death (getting his death), ditch.

groodles   *n (pl.).* broken pieces of food mixed with liquid left at the bottom of a soup bowl, etc. Fitzmaurice, *F*, 96: "[T]is she is good. . . that's always giving us these groodles fine. . . ."

grug   *n.* hunkers. [< Ir. *grog,* haunch.] Sayers, *P*, 98: "She was on her grug there all the while puffing away at the old pipe."

grype   see: gripe.

guard   see: garda.

gwal (gwaul, gabhail, goleen)   *n.* a quantity, an armful, as much as can be held between outstretched arms. [< Ir. *gabháil.*] Somerville and Ross, *RME*, 306: "[S]he withdrew, muttering something about another 'goleen o' turf' . . . ." See: een.

gypo see: gipo.

Hag of beara (Beare) see: cailleach.

haggard (haggart, hagyard) *n.* an enclosure at the back of a far-mhouse; a stack yard. [Comb. of hay + garth.] Campbell, *P*, 265: "Come to my haggard gate, my very doorstep." Fitzmaurice, *R*, 82: "You can see him below at the bottom of the haggart . . . ." [The term appears in A.I. literature as early as Jonathan Swift's *Irish Eloquence* (ca. 1735); *November Haggard* (1971), ed. Peter Kavanagh, is the uncollected prose and verse of Patrick Kavanagh (1904-1967).]

hagyard see: haggard.

half-mounted gentleman (half-mounted man, half sir) see: squireen.

hames, make a *s. phr.* a mess; from the difficulty the uninitiated have with the curved pieces (hames) of the harness of a draft horse to which the traces are attached. Flanagan, *T*, 10: "[I]f ever I try to write out a bit of it, I make a terrible hames of it." Joyce, *FW*, 93.15: "[T]hat fenemine Parish Poser, . . . umprumptu rightoway hames. . . ."

hand running (handrunning) *s. phr.* in succession. [Engl. dial.] O'Casey, *P*, 161: ". . . I don't know what we'd have done only for poor oul' Bessie; up with her for th' past three nights, hand runnin'." Joyce, *U*, 780: "[H]is wife is fucked. . . 5 or 6 times handrunning . . . ."

hanging-gale see: gale day.

hard word, the *s. phr.* a caution, a tip, inside information, a proposal, an unjust judgment, the sack. Joyce, *D*, 51: "Whenever any job was vacant a friend was always ready to give him the hard word." Somerville and Ross, *RM*, 123: "[I]t was but little under five years from that autumn evening on the river when I had said what is called in Ireland 'the hard word,'" to that day in August when I was led to the altar by my best man . . . ." Gregory, *SP*, 102: "Oh, Denis, my heart is broken you to have died with the hard word upon you!"

harps see: head or harp.

Harrier see: Broy Harrier.

harvest, broken see: broken harvest.

hawnawm see: manim an diouol.

hazard *n.* a cab-stand. Joyce, *U*, 76: "Mr Bloom went round the corner and passed the drooping nags of the hazard."

head or harp *s. phr.* the Irish equivalent of head or tail: Irish coins, prior to the assimilation of Irish currency with British on January 5, 1826, had the British monarch's head on one side and the Irish harp surmounted by a crown on the other. O'Casey, *P*, 148: "PETER: Heads, a juice. / FLUTHER: Harps, a tanner." See: juice, tanner. [The term is cur., because the post-independence coins, introduced

in 1928 (W. B. Yeats was chairman of the coinage committee), re-
tained the harp, the traditional and official symbol of the Irish state.]
hear one's (our, their, your) ears, can't   see: can't hear one's ears.
hedge   see: ditch.
hedge (fodeen) school   *n.* a school established in response to the
suppression of legal means of education for Catholics in Ireland, first
under Cromwell and later under the Penal Code introduced at the
end of the 17th c.; from the initial location of such schools in the
secrecy of hedges. Joyce, *FW*, 533.26-27: "[O]ne of my life's ambi-
tions . . . from an early peepee period while still to hedjeskool. .
. ." Cross, *T*, 57: "In my time there was no national school. Only
the 'fodeen', the hedge school." See: national school. [Hedge schools
were illegal until the passing of the Catholic Emancipation Act in
1829, but lasted until the middle of the 19th c., when they were replaced by the so-called national schools. They were also known as fodeen schools (< Ir. *fóidín*, a small sod); from the practice of pupils
having to supply such necessities as sods of turf for fires in winter.
The most notable writer in English to be educated in a hedge school
was William Carleton, and the "The Hedge School" is one of his
stories. Patrick Weston Joyce, author *of English as we speak it in
Ireland* (1910), received his early education in hedge schools, and
later became a teacher and an important administrator in the national school system. Red Hanrahan, in "Stories of Red Hanrahan"
(1897), by W. B. Yeats, is a hedge schoolmaster, whose school is
located in an old lime-kiln. The main setting of *Translations* (1980),
by Brian Friel, is a Donegal hedge school conducted in a disused barn
or hay shed in 1833, and the replacement of the hedge schools by
the national schools is one of a number of "translations" in the play;
The Hedge Schools of Ireland (1935, rev. 1968) is a study of the subject by P. J. Dowling.]
heirna (bierna, chiernah, Thighearna, Tierna), oh (a)   *excl., voc.,
n.* my Lord (God); my Master (temporal). [< Ir. *a Thighearna*.]
Fitzmaurice, *F*, 3: "And, oh hierna! the heart is rising in me. . . ."
Fitzmaurice, *R*, 95: "Oh bierna! to be married by a suspended priest
to boot."
hen, the old   see: old hen.
herself   *n.* housewife, mistress. Joyce, *FW*, 363.07: "The boss made
dovesandraves out of his bucknesst while herself wears the bowler's
hat in her bath." [*Herself Surprised* is a film script by Hugh
Leonard.]
hike   *interj.* a command to a horse to halt. Joyce, *FW*, 377.23:
"[H]ike, here's the hearse and four horses . . . ."
hillsiders (hillside men, mountainy men)   *n (pl.).* poor farmers,

rebels; from the fact that the dispossessed Irish were driven into marginal hillside lands during the various plantations. Joyce, *D*, 125: "Some of these hillsiders and fenians are a bit too clever if you ask me. . . ." See: Fenian; cf. sky farmer. [*Hillsiders* (1909) is a collection of short stories by Seamus O'Kelly.]

himself *n.* the householder, manager, boss, husband. Joyce, *FW*, 197.32: "But where was Himself, the timoneer?" Cf. herself.

hise *v.* to lift. [H.E. var. of Engl. dial. hoise.] Corkery, *S*, 112: "[W]at's to hinder us giving her a hise up in the morning when we're fresh?"

hold your hour   see: hour, hold (take) your

hold your whisht (whishth, whist, wheesht, whuisht)   see: whisht.

holy alls   *s. phr.* the end. Joyce, *D*, 154: "O, he'll do for himself one day and that's the holy alls of it."

holy hour, the   *s. phr.* the period in the afternoon from 2:30 to 3:30 when the pubs of Dublin closed (iron.); from a Catholic religious observance known as a Holy Hour. Beckett, *MU*, 30: "Needle knows no holy hour." [To be allowed to remain in a pub during the holy hour was a sign of special status. The institution of the holy hour is the focus of *Jaysus Wept* (1984), by Pete St. John. It was abolished, except on Sunday, under the provisions of the Intoxicating Liquor Bill, 1988.]

hon (hone), oh   see: ochone.

honam (honamaundhiaoul)   see: manim an dioul.

hooker   *n.* a wooden, gaff-rigged sloop, with a long bow-sprit and tan sails, used for transporting goods along the west coast of Ireland. Synge, *R*, 7: "[T]he tide's turning at the green head, and the hooker's tacking from the east." [A few hookers have been preserved as pleasure craft and have made major ocean voyages; "The Last Galway Hooker" is a poem by Richard Murphy (1927-).]

hooley   *n.* a traditional, uninhibited Irish party or celebration, usu. involving drinking, singing and dancing. [Perh. < hoolee, the Hindu vernal festival, or Ir. *hulach*, commotion, uproar.] O'Casey, *S*, 11: "[T]here is nothing' I'm more fond of than a Hooley." [Many Irishmen served in the Br. Army in India.]

horn of a bull, hoof of a horse, (snarl of a dog), smile of a Saxon (Englishman)   *prov.* three (four) things of which an Irishman should beware. Joyce, *U*, 23. "Horn of a bull, hoof of a horse, smile of a Saxon." O'Casey, *PD*, 404. "[T]hrough the roads of the four green fields goes Shane the Proud, with his fine head hidden, waving away his more venturesome friends from the horns of a bull, the hoofs of a horse, the snarl of a dog, an' the smile of an Englishman." See: four green fields. [Shane (the Proud) O'Neill was an Uls. chieftain in the 16th c.]

hoult   *n.* a grasp. [H.E. var. of hold.] Sayers, *P*, 51: "The bad times had a firm hoult of the poor people . . . ." [A fine hoult is a s. phr. for a sexually attractive person.]

hour, hold (take) your   *s. phr.* stay, relax, wait a while. O'Casey, *J*, 100: "Take your hour, there, take your hour!" [*Hold your hour and have another* (1963) is a collection of articles first published by Brendan Behan in *The Irish Press.*]

houseen   *n.* a little house (end.); a shed. [house + een, H.E. dim. suf. < Ir. *ín*.] Synge, *P*, 89:" [Y]ou'd have a right to come on, young fellow, till you see my little houseen, a perch off on the rising hill." See: een.

how are you (how-are-yeh)   *interj.* placed at the end of a statement to indicate iron. Joyce, *E*, 16: "Brigid, *laughs heartily:'* Practice, how are you!' " Cf. inagh, moryah. ["Fishermen — How are Yeh" (1977) is a poem by Pearse McLoughlin.]

huist   see: be dhe husth.

hullagone   see: ullagone.

hungry grass (fair gurtha, faragurtha)   *n.* a patch of mountain grass supposed to cause incapacitating attacks of hunger when walked upon (folk.); a sudden attack of hunger. [< Ir. *féar gorta*, hungry grass.] Yeats, *M*, 224: "He is eating as if he had trodden on the hungry grass." Maxwell, *W*, 218: "The *faragurta* comes on suddenly — a general weakness precedes the attack — the sufferer's strength is prostrated in an instant — he sinks down, and, if assistance is not at hand, perishes." [The effects of the hungry grass can be avoided, it is said, by carrying food and cured by a grain of oats. In "The Rival Kempers", a story by William Carleton, the power of the hungry grass is attributed to a curse of the fairies; "The Hungry Grass" is a poem by Donagh MacDonagh (1912-1968), and a novel (1969) by Richard Power (1928-1970).]

hurley (hurly, hurling, hurl, hurle, hurling stick)   *n., v.* a Gaelic game played with a curved wooden stick (*cáman*), which is used to strike a leather ball (*sliotar*); the stick used in the game; to play the game. Gregory, *SP*, 116: "It was I won at the hurley!" *Ibid.*, 193: "It may be they have need of my strength to help them in their hurling and their wars." Gregory, *SP*, 116: "Take this hurl, this silver ball." O'Grady, *B*, 45: "He had brought his ball and hurle of red-bronze with him . . . ." Cf. caman. ["A Boy Hurling on a Spring Day" is a poem by Daniel Corkery. Because of their size and shape, hurleys were sometimes used instead of rifles by insurgents in training exercises or in guards of honour during the struggle for independence, and at one stage were proscribed by Br. authorities.]

Hy Brasail   see: I Bhreasail.

I Bhreasail (Hy Brasail) *n.* an Elysium somewhere west of Ireland in the Atlantic Ocean. [Ir. *I Breasail.*] Corkery, *I*, 72, "My visions . . . spy far off on the ocean's rim / The peaks of I Bhreasail purple and dim!" Griffin, *H*, 152: "On the ocean that hollows the rocks where ye dwell, / A shadowy land has appeared, as they tell; / Men thought it a region of sunshine and rest, / And they called it Hy-Brasail, the isle of the blest." [*I Bhreasail* (1921) is a book of lyrics by Daniel Corkery; "Hy-Brasail" is a popular poem by Gerald Griffin. Hy Brasail is one of the *Insulae Purpuraricae* described by Pliny; geographers and cartographers were so convinced of its existence that it was shown on some charts issued as late as 1853; it is sometimes identified with the most famous mythical island, Atlantis.]

Iar (Jar) *a.* West (only used in the context of Connacht). [Ir. *Iar.*] Gregory, *SP*, 220: "Asking help he was for the people of Iar Connacht that are down under the fever and the famine."

idjeet (ijit) see: eejit.

ikey *a.* clever, cunning (sl.). [Br. sl.] Joyce, *U*, 57: "Ikey touch that: homerule sun rising up in the northwest."

illilo see: alilu.

in it *s. phr.* alive, existing, there. [< Ir. *ann.*] Joyce, *D*, 16: "[W]e wouldn't see him want anything while he was in it."

in my back see: back, in my

in the pay of the Castle see: pay of the castle.

inagh (inyah) *interj.* expressing dissent, disbelief or iron., usu. placed at the end of a statement. [< Ir. *An eadh?* Is that so?] Joyce, *U*, 427: "High angle fire, inyah!" Cf. how are you, moryah.

inch *n.* a long strip of level grassy land along a river. [< Ir. *inis.*] Corkery, *S*, 124: "[T]he sudden downpour of rain towards the end of August swept his newly-gathered cruach of turf from the inches, leaving him without fuel for the coming year. . . ." See: cruach. [*The Recluse of Inchidony* (1830) is a poem by Jeremiah Joseph Callanan (1795-1829).]

Inisfail (Innisfail, Fal) *n.* Ireland (lit.). [Ir. *Inis Fáil*, Island of Fal (a ritual stone at Tara).] Joyce, *U*, 293: "In Inisfail the fair there lies a land, the land of holy Michan." Pearse, *P*, 332: "Gráinne Mhaol is coming from over the sea / The Fenians of Fál as a guard about her. . . ." See: Granuaile (Gráinne Mhaol), Fenian; cf. Inishfallen. ["The Sorrows of Innisfail" is a poem by James Clarence Mangan; "Song of Innisfail" is one of the *Irish Melodies* (1808) of Thomas Moore (1779-1852); "Adieu to Innisfail" is a song by Richard D'Alton Williams (1822-1862); *Innisfail, a Lyrical Chronicle of Ireland* (1862) is a volume by Aubrey De Vere (1814-1902).]

Inishfallen (Innisfallen)   *n.* Ireland (lit.); after an island in the lower lake of Killarney. [< Ir. *Inis Faithleann.*] O'Casey, *A, II*, 247: "Sweet Inishfallen, fare thee well! Forever!" Cf. Inisfail. [*The Annals of Inishfallen*, covering the history of Ireland from the earliest times to 1326, were compiled in a monastery on the island; "Sweet Innisfallen" is one of the *Irish Melodies* (1808) of Thomas Moore (1779-1852); *Inishfallen, Fare Thee Well* (1949) is the fourth of six books of autobiography by Sean O'Casey; "Sweet Inishfallen, Fare Thee Well" is a section of *Rich and Rare: A Book of Ireland* (1984) by Sean McMahon (1931-).]

innis (inish, innish)   *n.* an island: com. in place-names. [< Ir. *inis.*] Yeats, *PO*, 44: "I will arise and go now, and go to Innisfree. . . ." O'Casey, *A, II*, 247: "Sweet Inishfallen, fare thee well! Forever!" Synge, *PO*, 37: "Bring Kateen-beug and Maura Jude / To dance in Beg-Innish. . . ." See: een, Inishfallen; beg (beug). ["Sweet Innishfallen" is one of the *Irish Melodies* (1808) of Thomas Moore (1779-1852); "Beg-Innish" is a poem by J. M. Synge; "The Lake Isle of Innisfree" is a poem by W. B. Yeats; *Inishfallen, Fare Thee Well* is a section of *Rich and Rare: A Book of Ireland* (1984) by Sean McMahon (1931-); Inishmore is the largest of the three Aran Island in Galway Bay.]

intill   *prep.* into (Uls.). [Uls. var. of into.] Ferguson, *P*, 93: "[D]rive the rebels would dar' to raise / The Irish colours, intill the says!"

inver   *n.* an inlet, an estuary. [< Ir. *inbhear.*] Colum, *PC*, 139: "[F]rom the cairns of Galway / To the invers of Cork it sparkled and shone . . . ." [Inver is a river and village in Larne, Co. Antrim; Inveran is a village in Co. Galway; the word also appears in Scottish place-names such as Inverness; *The Big House of Inver* (1925) is a novel by E. Œ. Somerville and Martin Ross; see: Big House.]

Inyah   see: inagh.

Iosa   *n.* Jesus. [Ir. *Íosa.*] Joyce, *FW*, 526.25: "[T]he Lord, with . . . his bouchel Iosa. . . ." See: bouchal (bouchel). [*Íosagan* (Little Jesus) is a story and a play by Patrick Pearse.]

iron fool   *s. phr.* one who pretends to be a fool in order to obtain some advantage. Sayers, *P*, 120: "He'd pretend to be a fool, but the people knew that Pléasc was what is called an 'iron fool.' " [There is an obvious pun on the term in the title of *The Green Fool* (1938), an autobiographical work by Patrick Kavanagh (1904-1967); he uses the phr. iron fool and explains it in his novel *Tarry Flynn* (1948).]

Irregular   *n.* a soldier of the Irish Republican Army during the period of the Civil War (1922-23), between supporters and opponents of the Anglo-Irish Treaty (1921), which established the Irish Free State. Yeats, *PO*, 229: "An affable Irregular, / A heavily-built Falstaffian man, / Comes cracking jokes of civil war / As though to die by gunshot were / The finest play under the sun." Cf. Diehard, Stater. [The IRA opposed the treaty because it provided a limited measure of independence, partitioned Ireland into two states, the Irish Free State and Northern Ireland, and required an oath of allegiance to the Br. Crown.]

Island (Land) of Saints and Sages (Scholars) *c. phr.* Ireland (lit., hist.). O'Casey, *S*, 81: "The land of Saints and Scholars 'ill shortly be a land of bloody poets." [The phr. emerged in the medieval period, and there is, according to the historian F. X. Martin, O.S.A., "a substantial basis for Ireland's grandiose title, 'the island of saints and scholars', which patriots repeated in later centuries and in darker days." *The Isle of Saints* is a play by St. John Greer Ervine (1883-1971); "Ireland, Island of Saints and Sages" is an essay by James Joyce; *Saints, Scholars and Schizophrenics* (1979) is a study of mental illness in rural Ireland by N. Scheper-Hughes. Given the recent political and social history of Ireland, the phrase is now occ. used ironically.]

Jack Latten see: dance Jack Latten.

Jackeen *n.* a Dubliner (pej.); used mostly in rural areas. [Jack + H.E. dim. suf. een (< Ir. *ín*).] Joyce, *P*, 93: ". . . Peter Pickackafax beside him was his eldest son but . . . he was only a Dublin jackeen." [In the Engl. of Newfoundland, a Jackeen is a rascally boy.]

Janey Mac, the child's a black see: Jesus Jack the child is black.

Jar see: Iar.

jar *n.* an alcoholic drink (sl.). O'Casey, *S*, 11: "[H]e's talk from morning till night when he has a few jars in him." ["On the jar" is a drinking spree.]

Jaysus (Jayshus, Jaysis, Jayzus, Jasus, Jazus) *n., excl.* Jesus. [18th c. Engl. pron. com. in H.E.] Joyce, *SH*, 113. "Doesn't he look like a wirrasthrue Jaysus? said Stephen pointing to the Tsar's photograph and using the Dublin version of the name as an effective common noun." Gogarty, *A*, 42: "The plainer Dubliners amaze us / By their so frequent use of 'Jayshus!' / Which makes me entertain the notion / It is not always from devotion." O'Casey, *C*, 387: "Jasus, you have lovely eyes!" Irvine, *L*, 92: "Jazus! . . . it's snowin." See: wirasthrue. [*Jaysus Wept* (1984) is the story of a "holy hour" in a Dublin pub by Pete St. John; see: holy hour. As the quot. from Oliver St. John Gogarty's *As I Was Going Down Sackville Street* (1937) suggests, Jaysus is considered a *sine qua non* in representations of Dublin speech.]

Jesus Jack (Janey Mac) the child is black (Janey Mac) *c. phr., interj.* expresses surprise; obvious, given the rarity of black people in

Ireland. Joyce, *U*, 742: "[T]he one they called budgers or something like a nigger with a shock of hair on it Jesus jack the child is black . . . ."

jigs on the green   see: wigs on the green.

jills   see: gills.

jinnyjo (Ginny Joe)   *n*. thistledown and seed, such as dandelion, floating in the air. Joyce, *FW*, 526.17: "You're forgetting the jinny-jos for the fayboys."

Johnny Magorey / McGory (magories)   *n*. a hip, a dog-haw, the berry of the dog-rose; a rhyme used to tease young children. [Perh. < Ir. *mucóir*, a haw.] Joyce, *U*, 174: "If you didn't know risky putting anything into your mouth. Poisonous berries. Johnny Magories." Crosbie, *D*, 57: "Will I tell you a story? / About Johnny Magories? / Will I begin it? / That's all that's in it." Pearse, *P*, 73: ". . . I thrashed him ere-yesterday for putting magories down my neck!" [The term appears, lightly disguised, in Joyce's *Finnegans Wake*: "the jolly magorios . . ." (454.15); the Crosbie quot. is the rhyme used to tease young children with the promise of a story that is not told; Ballymagorry is a village in Co. Derry.]

joult   *n*., *v*. a journey, esp. one which is long or rough. [Var. of jolt.] Joyce, *U*, 750: "[H]e was making free with me after the Glencree dinner coming back that long joult over the featherbed mountain . . . ." Joyce, *FW*, 47.07: "He was joulting by Wellington's monument . . . ."

Jubilee mutton   *c. phr*. very little (iron., Dub.); from the distribution of small quantities of free mutton to the poor of Dublin during the celebration of Queen Victoria's Diamond Jubilee in 1897. Joyce, *U*, 427: "What's he got? Jubilee mutton." Cf. Famine Queen.

juice   see: deuce.

junk   *n*. a chunk; a large piece, esp. of bread (col.). Corkery, *S*, 46: "[H]e broke off some junks and began hastily to chew them . . . ."

kailecannon (kale-canon)   see: colcannon.

kam   see: cam.

Kathleen [ni Houlihan]   see: Cathleen ni Houlihan.

kead millia failta   see: cead mille failte.

keen (keenthecaun)   *v*., *n*. to lament for the dead, to wail; the traditional lament for the dead. [< Ir. *caoineadh*.] Synge, *R*, 25: "I'll have no call now to be going down and getting Holy Water in the dark nights after Samhain, and I won't care what way the sea is when the other women will be keening." See: Samhain; cf. caoine. ["Owen Reilly: a Keen" is a poem by James Clarence Mangan; "A Woman of the Mountain Keens Her Son" is a poem by Patrick Pearse.]

keener   *n.* a woman employed to keen at a wake or funeral. See: keen. ["The Keening Woman" is a story by Patrick Pearse.]

keeping, on his (my)   *s. phr.* on the run, fugitive. Joyce, *FW*, 191.11-12: "There grew up beside you . . . an unwashed savage, on his keeping and in yours . . . ." Corkery, *H*, 9: "I was on the run, or, in the phrase that goes through so many centuries of Irish history, I was on my keeping." [The phr. appears in print as early as 1668.]

keeroge   see: ciarog.

kern (kearne)   *n.* a lightly-armed, Irish foot-soldier, a rebel (hist., lit.); a rich, vulgar clown (rare). [< Ir. *ceithirn.*] Campbell, *P*, 215: "But most, / Trooped in the country folk: poor kerns, / Wild in shag rugs (so Derrek's pen / Drew them), with glibbs of matted hair . . . ." See: glib. [The term appears in literature as early as Shakespeare's *King Richard II.*]

Kildare side   *s. phr.* the right-hand side of the head. Joyce, *FW*, 516. 03-06: "[H]e come up, . . . got up regardless, with a cock on the Kildare side of his Tattersull . . . ."

kill the Danes, that would   see: Danes.

kind (kind father/mother)   *a., s. phr.* natural, inherited from the father or mother. Corkery, *H*, 15: " 'Tis kind for him to be like that . . . ." Somerville and Ross, *B*, 218: "Kind father for him! What's bred in the bone will come out in the meat." *Ibid.*, 199: "Kind mother for her!" [Kind father appears in A.I. literature as early as *A Dialogue in Hibernian Style* (ca. 1735) by Jonathan Swift (1667-1745).]

kinnatt (cnat)   *n.* a rogue, an impertinent little person (pej.). [< Ir. *cnat.*] Joyce, *U*, 363: "[S]he was simply in a towering rage though she hid it, the little kinnatt . . . ." [The term appears in Joyce's *Finnegans Wake* lightly disguised as "kennet" (213.11).]

kip (kip-shop)   *n.* a hovel, a brothel, an unpleasant place (sl., pej.). [<Dan. *horekippe*, brothel.] Joyce, *U*, 15: "Hurry out to your school kip and bring us back some money." *Ibid.*, 328: "We too, she said, will seek the kips where shady Mary is." [Dublin's notorious red-light district was called the kips and is setting of the "Circe" episode of Joyce's *Ulysses; I'm Getting Out of this Kip* (1968) is a play by Heno Magee (1939-).]

kippeen (kippen, kippin, cipen, cipin)   *n.* a little stick; a kindling stick; a skewer; the stick used to play a bodhran (goatskin drum); a cudgel used in faction fighting (end.). [<Ir. *cipín.*] Yeats, *PL*, 97: "Give me the loan of a kippeen to stir the pot with . . . ."

kish (kishogue)   see: cish.

kitchen (kitshen)   *n.* any condiment or relish, such as salt, butter or dripping, eaten with potatoes and other plain foods. Gregory, *SP*, 90: "[A]s to the sea, there is something from it every day of the year, a

handful of periwinkles to make kitchen, or cockles maybe."
["Hunger is good kitchen" (prov.).]
kithog (kithogue, kitthoge, ciotog)   *n., a.* the left hand, left-handed,
a left-handed person; occ. left-legged. [< Ir. *ciotóg*.] Joyce, *U*, 429:
"Kithogue! Salute." Joyce, *FW*, 91.34: "[T]he halfkneed castle-
knocker's attempting kithoguishly to lilt his holymess and the paws and
make the sign of the Roman Godhilic faix . . . ." See: faiks (faix).
["Ciotóg" is the nic. of a character in *Peig* (1936), the autobiography
in Ir. of Peig Sayers; Kithogue is an off-stage character in *The King of
Friday's Men* (1948), a play by M. J. Molloy (1917-1994);"As sharp
as a ciotog" (c. phr.).]
kitshen   see: kitchen.
Lamh Dearg Abu (Lamh Dearg an Oughter)   *slog.* Red Hand [of
Ulster] to Victory, or Uppermost: the slog. of the O'Neill family. [Ir.
Lámh Dearg Abú (Lámh Dearg an Uachtair).] Joyce, *U*, 325:" [T]hen
lifted he in his rude great brawny strengthy hands the medher of dark
strong foamy ale and, uttering his tribal slogan *Lamh Dearg Abu*, he
drank to the undoing of his foes. . . ." See: medher.
Land of Youth   see: Tir na nOg.
lanna, a   see: alanna.
Lanna Mochree's dog,   see: Lanty McHale's dog.
lannan shee (linnaun shee, leananshee)   *n.* a fairy that falls in love with
a mortal. [< Ir. *leannán sídh,* fairy lover.] Colum, *PC*, 103: "The
Lannan Shee / Watched the young man Brian. . . ." Fitzmaurice, *F*, 52:
"Foola, Jamsie Kennelly, blinded by an old vagabone's chicanery, an
old toothless hag, and she surely no Linnaun Shee." Campbell, *L*, 225:
" [L]ike a lovesick leananshee, / She hath my heart in thrall." See: shee,
foola. [*The Linnaun Shee* (1924) is a one-act comedy by George Fitzmaurice, and the name of a character in the play.]
**Lanty McHale's dog / goat, like (Lanna Mochree's dog, Dolan's ass,
Tom Trot's dog)**   *c. phr.* a time-server, one who is anxious to please
and agrees with every point of view (pej.). Joyce, *SH*, 112: "Protestant
Orthodoxy is like Lanty McHale's dog: it goes a bit of the road with
everyone." Joyce, *U*, 336: "Gob he's like Lanty MacHale's goat that'd
go a piece of the road with every one."
laogh, a   *voc.,* my dear (end.). [Ir. *laogh,* a suckling calf, a term of
end.).] Corkery, *S*, 50: " '[W]hisper, *a laogh,*' he drew the woman
towards him."
lashings   *n.* plenty; esp. food and drink (sl.). Joyce, *U*, 234: "Lashings
of stuff we put up: port wine and sherry and curaçao to which we
did ample justice."
lather (leather)   *v.* to beat, to do something with vigour. [Perh.
< Ir. *leadradh,* striking, whipping.] Joyce, *FW*, 200.34: "Tell me the

trent of it while I'm lathering hail out of Denis Florence MacCar-
thy's combies." [MacCarthy (1817-1882): a prolific minor poet,
translator and professor of English at the Catholic University,
Dublin.]

lawn   see: cruiskeen (lawn).

lazy-beds   *n (pl.).* wide raised beds for cultivating potatoes formed by placing rows of seed-potatoes on top of the sod and covering
them by folding over the sod between the beds. Somerville and Ross,
RME, 180: "An old woman was digging at the other side of the field,
and I steered for her, making a long tack down a deep furrow between the 'lazy-beds'." [This labour-saving method of cultivation has
the added advantage of forming trenches between the beds which
provide drainage; "Lazy-Beds" is a chapter in *Irish Folk Ways* (1957)
by E. Estyn Evans.]

leaca   *n.* the side of a hill, a flat sloping surface, a spur of land jut-
ting out from the side of a mountain. [Ir. *leaca*.] Corkery, *S*, 260:
"[H]e passed a lonely farm-house clung against its slab of protec-
ting rock at the base of a cliff, or espied one aloft on some *leaca*
or other. . . ." ["The Ploughing of Leaca-na-Naomh" (L. of the
Saints) is the first short story in *A Munster Twilight* (1916), a collection by Daniel Corkery.]

leananshee   see: lannan shee.

leanav   see: alanna.

leathan   *a.* wide. [Ir. *leathan*.] Yeats, *M*, 113: "[H]e's leathan
(wide) and not smart."

lebidin (libidjeh)   *n.* an awkward, blundering, half fool (pej.). [<
Ir. *leibide*, an awkward clown, an idiot.] Hyde, *T*, 146: "[T]he great
trouble of the world directed him among the *leibidins* of the province of Munster . . . ."

leg of   see: great leg of.

libidjeh   see: lebidin.

**like Lanty McHale's dog / goat (Lanna Mochree's dog, Dolan's ass,
Tom Trot's dog)**   see: Lanty McHale's dog.

linn   *n.* a pool, a pond, a lake. [Ir. *linn*.] Colum, *PO*, 116: ". .
. I think upon your converse kind by the meadow / And the linn
. . . ." [The word is part of the name of Dublin in Engl. (*Dubhlinn*,
Blackpool).]

linnaun shee   see: lannan shee.

linney (linnhe)   *n.* a storage shed attached to a farm house. [Var.
of Engl. dial. linhay, an open-fronted farm building.] Fitzmaurice,
F, 27: "That snarl was for himself, out in the linnhe, the chronic!"

liss (lios)   *n.* a rath, a ring-fort. [< Ir. *lios*.] Yeats, *M*, 61: "[F]oxes
and cats like, above all, to be in the 'forths' and lisses after night-

fall . . . ." Corkery, *S*, 96: "We gathered to the *lios*, the gentry mak-ing their own of the raised ground within it." [Liss is a com. prefix in place names, such as Lissadell, Co. Sligo and Lissdoonvarna, Co. Clare.]

litis   *a*. white. [Ir. *lítis*, white, the white colour of skin or fur.] Cor-kery, *S*, 94: "She was called Litis because she was a cold sort of white, without a tint of warmth in it." See: tint.

Little Black (Dark) Rose   see: Dark Rosaleen.

little people   see: gentle folk.

llanuv, ma   see: alanna.

loan of, a   *s. phr.* an influence on. Joyce, *D*, 129: "He's not a bad sort, said Mr Henchy, only Fanning has such a loan of him."

lob (lop)   *n.* a quantity, especially of money (Cork); a lump (pej.). [Engl. dial.] Joyce, *P*, 93: "To the sellers in the market, to the barmen and barmaids, to the beggars who importuned him for a lob Mr Dedalus told the same tale. . . ."

Lochlann (Lochlanach)   *n.* Scandinavia, a Norseman, a Dane (lit.). [< Ir. *Lochlannach*.] Gregory, *SP*, 177: "[M]y father, before go-ing to Lochlann, said he must leave me in a husband's care." Joyce, *U*, 45: "Galleys of the Lochlanns ran here to beach, in quest of prey, their bloodbeaked prows riding low on a molten pewter surf." Gregory, *SP*, 223: "Did you ever hear the news of the families that drove out the Danes, the Lochlanach, from Ireland?"

lock   *n.* a quantity, a bundle, an armful. [Engl. dial.] Hyde, *T*, 146: "I'll bring in a lock of hay."

long car   see Bianconi.

lood (lude)   *a.* ashamed. [< Ir. *lúd*.] Joyce, *FW*, 469.21: "Lood Erynnana, ware the wail!" See: Eire (Erynnana).

looderamawn (loodheramaun, luderamaun, luderman, ludhramaun, ludraman)   *n.* a lazy, idle person; a lout; a fool (pej.). [< Ir. *ludramán*.] Joyce, *U*, 305: ". . . Pisser Burke told me there was an old one there with a cracked loodheramaun of a nephew . . . ." Joyce, *FW*, 21.30: "[S]he convorted him to the oneshure allgood and he became a luderman." See: old one. [The word also appears, somewhat heavily disguised, in an excl. in Joyce's *Finnegans Wake*: "Uploudermainagain!" (358.19).]

lop   see: lob.

loppeen   *n.* the leg of a goose or other fowl. [< Ir. *lóipín*, white stocking (of a bird).] Fitzmaurice, *F*, 23: "[T]he baisht would turn around from the table there and, shameless to the world, call for the six lopeens." See: een.

lost green field   see: four green fields.

loy   *n.* a heavy-bladed, one-eared spade, with a heel of wood protruding from the back of the shaft for extra leverage, used for cultivating potatoes. [< Ir. *láighe*.] Synge, *P*, 73: "I just riz the loy and let fall the edge of it on the ridge of his skull. . . ." [Most common in counties bordering the middle and upper Shannon, big loys, veritable foot-ploughs, were sometimes so heavy that they were dragged along the ground, rather than carried. The weight of a loy is suggested in Synge's play, *The Playboy of the Western World*, in which Christy Mahon, quoted above, boasts that he "killed" his father by letting a loy fall on his skull.]

luck-money (penny)   *n.* a token sum of money returned to the buyer by the seller at the conclusion of a transaction, so that the buyer will have luck with the purchase. Somerville and Ross, *RM*, 52: ". . . I sold the Bandon horse for £75 to old Welply, and I had to give him back a couple of sovereigns luck-money." Somerville and Ross, *A*, 39: "[W]ould ye be willing to give twenty pounds for the mare, and he to give back a pound luck-penny?"

luderamaun (luderman, ludraman)   see: loodheramaun.

luss (lusmore, lus-mor, fairy-cap)   *n.* foxglove, *Digitalis purpurea*: a potent plant in fairy lore, sometimes called fairy-cap, fairy-finger or fairy-thimble. [< Ir. *lus (na mban sídhe)*, banshees' plant, or *lusmór*, great plant.] Campbell, *P*, 52: "I have gathered *luss* / At the wane of the moon, / And supped its sap / With a yellow spoon." *Ibid.*, 26: "And what did I then / Let no mouth say, / For I tied God's cow / To a lusmore spray." Gregory, *P*, 91: "To bring anyone back from being with the fairies, you should get the leaves of the *Lus-mor*, and give them to him to drink." [The foxglove is sometimes called a gentle plant; see: gentle and gentle folk: Lusmore is the nic. of the hunchback in "The Legend of Knockgrafton" by T. Crofton Croker (1798-1845).]

m'anam ón diabhal   see: manim an diouol.

maam   see: mam.

mabhron   see: mavrone.

mac, a   see: avic.

machree (mo chree, achree, a-chree, ma-cree)   *voc., n.* my heart, my love (end.). [< Ir. *a (mo) chroidhe*, my heart.] Joyce, *U*, 287: "Ben machree, said Mr Dedalus, clapping Ben's fat back shoulderblade." O'Casey, *R*, 275: "An whenever he sung 'Mother Mo Chree', wasn't there a fewroory in Heaven with the rush that was made to lean over and hear him singin' it." ["Acushala Gal Machree" is a song; "Mother Machree' is a song by Samuel Lover (1797-1868); Widda Machree is a character in *Time To Go*, a one-act play by Sean O'Casey.]

macruiskeen   see: cruiskeen lawn.

macushla   see: acushla.

maddor   see: medher.

mag   *n.* a swoon. Corkery, *M*, 143: "[T] he second time the cries came outside her window, Miss Nora fell down in a dead mag — stiff to the world, and had to be lifted up to bed."

Magorey, Johnny   see: Johnny Magorey.

mahone, pogue   see: poguemahone.

make   *n.* a halfpenny (sl., Dub.); obs. since decimalization of currency in 1971. [Rare or obs. Engl. sl.] O'Casey, *S*, 21: "I haven't got a make." [One of the "abusive names" HCE is called in Joyce's *Finnegans Wake* is *"Tanner and a Make . . ."* (71.28); see: tanner.]

malavogue (mallavogue, malivogue, mal-a-voke)   *v.* to berate or curse. [Perh. < Ir. *mallacht*, to curse.] O'Casey, *S*, 21: ". . . I gave one ov them a mallavogin the other day for callin' him oul' hairpins!"

malt, ball of   see: ball of malt.

mam (maam)   *n.* a mountain pass. [Ir. *mám*.] Pearse, *P*, 8: "Often when I was at the *fosaidheacht* [herding cattle while they are grazing] he would come up into the green *mám* to me, with a little song he had made." Joyce, *FW*, 85.23: "[A] child of Maam, Festy King, ... was subsequently haled up at the Old Bailey. . . ." [Maam and Maam Cross are villages in Co. Galway.]

man in the gap [**of danger, death**]   *s. phr.* a hero, defender (lit.). [< Ir. *beárna baoghial*, gap of danger.] Joyce, *U*, 297: "[O]n these were graven . . . the tribal images of many Irish heroes and heroines of antiquity, Cuchulin . . . Christopher Columbus . . . The Man in the Gap . . . ." O'Casey, *C*, 384: "No, no, mine the gap of danger." Cf. barnabweel. [The Ir. phr. is in the refrain of "A Soldier's Song", the Irish national anthem: "Tonight we man the bearna baoghail / In Erin's cause come woe or weal . . . ."]

man of the house (farathee)   *n.* householder, master. [< Ir. *fear an tigh*, man of the house.] Joyce, *FW*, 101.32: "[B]ondswoman of the man of the house . . . ." ["The Man of the House" is a short story by Frank O'Connor.]

maneen (man-een)   *n.* a little man, a boy who tries to act like a man (pej.). [man + H.E. dim. suf. een (< Ir. *ín*).] Joyce, *P*, 92: "I was standing at the end of the South Terrace one day with some maneens like myself and sure we thought we were grand fellows because we had pipes stuck in the corners of our mouths." Somerville and Ross, *RME*, 285: "He asked me next morning, with a gallant attempt at indifference, if I had had any word of 'the man-een'." See: een.

manim an diouol (monamondiaoul, mon dhiol, hanam mo ndiabhail, hawnawm, honamaundhiaoul, honomaundhiaoul, m'anam ón diabhal, anamon dhoul, thonamon dux)   *excl.* my (your) soul from (to) the devil. [< Ir. *(tuar) m' (d') anam ón (don) diabhal.*] Corkery, *S*, 118: "Hawn — awm — she'd — be — a lovely sight by this down below . . . ." Somerville and Ross, *RM*, 275: "Howld to the stheel / Honamaundhiaoul; she'll run off like an eel!" Somerville and Ross, *RME*, 208: " 'Honomaundhiaoul! Sulluvan!' he shouted, with a full-blown burst of ferocity . . . ." Fitzmaurice, *R*, 99: "Anamon dhoul it's mad I'm going entirely." Fitzmaurice, *F*, 139: "Thonamon dux he to lay a hand on the Danagher chief!"

mankey (manky) *a.* filthy (sl.). [Br. sl.] Joyce, *FW*, 337.29: "[Y]our hahititahiti licks the mankey nuts!"

marin see: mering.

martheen see: Andrew Martins.

martyrdom, red (white) *s. phr.* death (red) or exile (white) for the faith. [Perh. < Ir. *dearg (bán) mhartra*.] Gregory, *B*, 29: "[H]e bade the brothers to have a mind prepared for red martyrdom and a mind strong and steadfast for white martyrdom. . . ." [There is an Ir. triad: *Trí cinéala martra: bán-mhartra, agus glas-mhartra agus dearg-mhartra.* Three kinds of martyrdom: white-martyrdom, green-martyrdom (imprisonment) and red-martyrdom; the word *glas* means a fetter (n.) and green (a.).]

mass see: meas.

massach *a.* having large hips, thighs or buttocks (pej.). [< Ir. *másach*.] Joyce, *FW*, 284.F4: "Braham Baruch he married his cook to Massach McKraw her uncle-in-law . . . ." Cf. mausey.

mausey (mawsy) *a.* having heavy buttocks, clumsy, ugly (pej.). [< Ir. *más*.] Joyce, *FW*, 127.32: "[He] plays gehamerat when he's ernst but misses mausey when he's lustyg . . . ." Leonard, *H*, 23: "Keep your mawsy hands to yourself." Cf. massach.

mavourneen (morneen, murneen, avourneen, savourneen, vourneen) *voc., n.* my love, darling (end.). [< Ir. *mo mhúirnín*, my darling, or *muirnín*, darling.] Joyce, *U*, 293: "Barney mavourneen's be it, says I." Hyde, *L*, 13: "I shall only marry my desire, / She is the morneen of the fair hair." ["Kathleen Mavourneen" (1830) is a popular love song by Julia Crawford (ca. 1799-1860; *Kathleen Mavourneen* (1898) is a novel by Randall William MacDonnell (1870-?); "Savourneen Deelish" is a love song; *Savourneen Dheelish* (1869) is a novel by Charles Anderson Read (1841-1878); "Eleanora Mavourneeen" is a chapter of *A Summer in Italy* (1950), a travel memoir by Sean O'Faolain.]

mavrone (mabhron) *excl.* alas. [< Ir. *mo bhrón*, my grief.] Joyce, *U*, 199: "And we to be there, mavrone, and you to be unbeknownst sending us your conglomerations the way we to have our tongues out a yard long like the drouthy clerics do be fainting for a pussful." See: do be, puss (pussful). [This quot. from Joyce's *Ulysses* is one of a number of parodies in the work of rendering of Irish folk speech by J. M. Synge and others.]

mawsy see: mausey.

McGory, Johnny   see: Johnny Magorey
McHale's dog (goat)   see: Lanty McHale's dog.
meal-monger   see: gombeen (man).
mearing   see: mering.
meas (mass)   *n.* respect, esteem. [Ir. *meas.*] Fitzmaurice, *F*, 90: "It is no mass at all then, you have on Ethne in the heel and is it the way you would leave her here in her lonesome in this fearsome land under the sea."
medher (mether, maddor)   *n.* a four-handled, square cup, usu. of wood. [< Ir. *meadar.*] Joyce, *U*, 325: "[T]hen lifted he in his rude great brawny strengthy hands the medher of dark strong foamy ale and, uttering his tribal slogan *Lamh Dearg Abu*, he drank to the undoing of his foes. . . ." See: Lamh Dearg Abu. [The term appears in A.I. literature as early as Jonathan Swift's *A Dialogue in Hibernian Style* (1735).]
mee-aw (meeraw)   *n.* bad luck, misfortune. [< Ir. *mí ádh* or *mí ráth.*] Somerville and Ross, *A*, 228: "Such a mee-aw! Such a thing to happen to me — the poor decent woman!"
mehill   see: meitheal.
meila (mela, millia) murder   *s. phr.* great noise, destruction, lamentation. [< Comb. of Ir. *míle*, thousand + murder.] Joyce, *U*, 329: "Then he was telling us the master at arms comes along with a long cane and he draws out and he flogs the bloody backside off the poor lad till he yells meila murder."
meitheal (mehill, mihil, mihul)   *n.* a work party, especially of reapers; the custom of providing a few days of assistance to neighbours during the harvest or turf-cutting period. [Ir. *meitheal.*] Fitzmaurice, *R*, 53: "There is a crowd of people on the road, and there is a mihil in Dan Curtin's field longside it." [The custom of providing such assistance to neighbours created a large circle of cooperation in a given district. Recipients of the assistance provided food and drink at the end of the work period, which was frequently followed by music, dancing and story telling; "as big as a blacksmith's meitheal" (s. phr.).]
mering (mearing, marin)   *n.* a well-marked boundary or fence between fields, bogs or farms. [Var. of rare or obs. Engl. mere (mear), a boundary.] Gregory, *SP*, 86: "It's a little temptation there was for my poor beasts to ask to cross the mering." Corkery, *S*, 54: "The sleeper might lawfully take his rest his spirit had so indisputably established itself everywhere within the far-flung mearings." Moore, *M*, 103: "[T]here is a fall into the marin stream betwixt your honour's property and the Miss Brennans'."
mhic, a   see: avic.

mhor (more) *a.* big, great: com. in names. [< Ir. *mór.*] Colum, *PO*, 49: "In the house of Fargel More . . . ." ["Mor of Cloyne" is a poem by Alfred Percival Graves (1846-1931); Gerald Fitzgerald, the Great Earl of Kildare (d. 1513), was known as Garret More; his sister, Eleanor, married Conn More O'Neill; Tullamore is a town in Co. Offaly.]

mich (mitch) *v.* to play truant, to sneak about. [Rare or obs. Engl. cur. in H.E.] Joyce, *D*, 21: "With Leo Dillon and a boy named Mahony I planned a day's miching." Synge, *P*, 111: "You're pot-boy in this place, and I'll not have you mitch off from us now." [The modern English phrase, "play truant," is a rarely used in Ireland; "The Mitcher" (1977) is a poem by Pearse McLoughlin.]

Mick *n., a.* Roman Catholic (pej., Uls.). McCabe, *C*, 534: "Wilson was a fly boy, and this Heath man's a bum boy, all them Tories is tricky whores, dale with Micks and Papes and lave us here to rot." [*A Mickrocosm of Ireland* is the iron. subtitle of *The Drums of Father Ned* (1959), a play by Sean O'Casey.]

micky (mickey) *n.* penis (sl., Dub.). Joyce, *U*, 780: ". . . Ill put on my best shift and drawers let him have a good eyeful out of that to make his micky stand for him . . . ."

micky dazzler *c. phr.* a "lady killer" (sl.). O'Casey, *J*,: "I saw yous comin' out of the Cornflower Dance class, an' you hangin' on his arm — a thin, lanky strip of a Micky Dazzler, with a walkin'-stick an' gloves!"

mihil (mihul) see: meitheal.

mille see: cead mille failte.

millia murder see: meila murder.

mind *v.* to heed, remember (Uls.). Joyce, *D*, 87: "Do you mind me now?" Irvine, *L*, 121: ". . . I want to mind it jist as Jamie and I saw it years an' years ago."

minnikin *n.* a very small pin. [Var. of minkin, rare or obs. Engl.] Joyce, *FW*, 207.14: "[A] request might she passe of him for a min-nikin."

minnshogue *n.* a young she-goat after first kidding. [< Ir. *minn-seog.*] Joyce, *FW*, 37.34: "[A] supreme of excelling peas, balled under minnshogue's milk . . . ."

mist that does be on the bog, the *c. phr.* applied to anything that smacks of the tendency to emphasize or idealize rural life in Ireland (pej.). Murphy, *C*, 33: ". . . Eileen Og, a girleen, how would you like to leave the mists that do be on the bog and fly away to make your fortune." See: Og, does be (do be), een. [*The Mist That Does Be on the Bog* (1909), a play by Gerald MacNamara (1866-1938), is a satire on this tendency in the Abbey Theatre.]

mitch see: mich.

moider (moidher, moither, myther) *v.* to annoy, irritate, or pester. Joyce, *FW*, 445.31: "[M]e far away on the pillow. . . whilst moidhered by the rattle of the doppeldoorknockers."

Monamondiaoul see: dhiol.

Month's Mind *s. phr.* a Mass and memorial service for the soul of an individual conducted a month after death. Macken, *SW*, 58: "He wasn't home until shortly before the Month's Mind for his father." [The phr. was used in England before the Reformation; it appears in Shakespeare's *Two Gentlemen of Verona*, I, ii, 134; *Lines Written in the Month's Mind of Mona Dunn. December 19, 1928 — January 19, 1929* (1929) is a volume by Shane Leslie (1875-1971).]

moonlighters *n (pl.).* tenant farmers who attacked the property and livestock of landlords in response to evictions, etc., during the period of the land war (1879-1903); their threats were issued over the signature, Captain Moonlight. Flanagan, *T*, 639: "Parnell's power lay not in the House, nor on Dublin or Cork platforms, but in the houghing blade of the moonlighter and the dynamite of the Fenian." See: Fenian. [*The Moonlighters* is a play (never produced) by George Fitzmaurice.]

more see: mhor.

More Irish than the Irish *c. phr.* the various invaders of Ireland, particularly the Anglo-Norman and early English, who, in time, became more Irish than the Irish themselves. [Perh. < L. *Hibernis ipsis Hiberniores*.] Joyce, *U*, 119: "More Irish than the Irish."

more power! (to your elbow / said old Power when when young Power was born) *c. phr.* of encouragement. Shaw, *J*, 407: "More power to your elbow! an may your shadda never be less! for youre the broth of a boy intirely." [This sentence contains what Shaw considered to be three typical, stage-Irish phrases; there may be some connection between more power and Power's Irish Whiskey, estd. in 1791, long before the term appears in print.]

morneen see: mavourneen.

Morra (Morrow) see: Gommorrah.

moryah (moryeah, moya, moyah, moy-ah) *interj.* indicates irony, dissent or disbelief, usu. placed at the end of a statement. [< Ir. *mar dheadh*, as it were.] Fitzmaurice, *F*, 22: "A hobby, moryah!" Joyce, *D*, 123. "[T]he men used to go in on Sunday morning before the houses were open to buy a waistcoat or a trousers — moya!" Cf. inagh, how are you.

mostha (mossa) see: musha.

mot (mott, motte) *n.* a girl; a girlfriend, wife; more recently, the heroine of a cowboy movie when used with the definite article (sl.,

Dub.). [Var. of mort, rare or obs. Engl. sl.] O'Casey, *J*, 131: "Never held a mot's hand, an' wouldn't know how to tittle a little Judy." Campbell, *P*, 257: "O, she'd make a mott for the provost Marshal, / or a wife for the Mayor on his coach so high . . . ." Beckett, *M*, 46: " 'Arragowan' she said 'make it four cantcher, yer frien', yer da, yet ma an' yer motte.' " See: arragowan.

mouldy   *a.* drunk (sl., Dub.). Joyce, *FW*, 128.02: "[T]hough he's mildewstained he's mouldystoned . . . ." See: stoned; cf. blue mouldy.

mountainy men   see: hillsiders.

moya (moyah, moy-ah)   see: moryah.

muddhaun   see: omadhaun.

Mullingar heifer, like a   see: beef to the heels.

murder an' ages   see: tare (and ages).

murneen   see: mavourneen.

Musha (Muise, Mostha, 'Sha, 'Usha, Wisha)   *interj.* Well, Indeed; usu. placed at the beginning of a sentence. [< Ir. *má 'seadh (muise).*] Joyce, *D*, 122: "Musha, God be with them times! said the old man." Pearse, *P*, 104: "They could, *muise.*" Somerville and Ross, *RME*, 233: " 'Sha! thim's no good to us!" Sayers, *P*, 81: " 'Sha, let's go on our knees in the name of God and say the rosary." Joyce, *D*, 123: " 'Usha, how could he be anything else?"

mwirra   see: wirra.

mythered   see: moidered.

N.T.   *abbr.* National Teacher: the holder of a national school teaching diploma earned at a teachers' training college. O'Casey, *J*, 66: "(*Signed*). . . Charles Bentham, NT". See: national school.

namplush   see: amplush.

napper   *n.* the head (sl.). [Engl. dial. and sl.] Fitzmaurice, *F*, 28: "[I]s it a gom I am to be bothering my napper with a poisoned whelp . . . ." See: gaum (gom).

national school   *n.* a school that was part of an educational system established in Ireland by the British Government in the middle of the 19th c. to replace the hedge schools. Fitzmaurice, *R*, 105: "I thought it was only the Inspector of National Schools was such a big fellow as that." See: hedge school. [Nationalists viewed the system and its curriculum, which excluded Irish history and the Irish language, as an attempt by the British to destroy Irish culture and assimilate the Irish. Patrick Pearse, leader of the 1916 Rising, attacked the system in *The Murder Machine* (1912). Patrick Weston Joyce, author of *English as we speak it in Ireland* (1910), who received his early education in hedge schools, later became a teacher and an important administrator in the national school system. The replacement of hedge schools by national schools is one of a number of "translations" in *Translations* (1980), a play by Brian Friel, most of which is set in a hedge school in 1833.]

nature   *n.* affection, affinity. Somerville and Ross, *B*, 258: "She'll often come in my little house — she has a nature for me, the crathur. . . ."

neither my arse nor my elbow   *c. phr.* neither one thing nor another (pej.). Joyce, *P*, 237: "Neither my arse nor my elbow! Temple cried scornfully. And that's what I call limbo."

nice (nicely)   *a., ad.* slightly intoxicated. Corkery, *M*, *125*: "After a while, when we were getting a little nice in ourselves, we began to find our tongues all right, and then there was talk and plenty of it . . . ."

nix, keep   *v.* to act as a lookout; term used esp. by children during such illicit activities as "boxing the fox" (stealing fruit from gardens or orchards). [Engl. sl.] Joyce, *D*, 126: "Her father used often to hunt them in out of the field with his blackthorn stick; but usually little Keogh used to keep *nix* and call out when he saw her father coming."

nod is as good as a wink (wink is as good as a nod — to a blind horse), a   *c. phr.* there is no need to say anything; I understand. O'Casey, *S*, 15: "You needn't say no more — a nod's as good as a wink to a blind horse . . . ." Irvine, *L*, 59: "Ah, ye hinted, an' a wink's as good as nod to a blind horse." [The phr. appears in Joyce's *Finnegans Wake* as "a nod to the nabir is better than a wink to the wabsanti" (5.21).]

noody-nady (noody-nahdy, noody-nawdy)   *a., n.* hesitant in speech, drunk; a person of insipid or annoying character. [< Ir. *niúdar neádar*.] Joyce, *FW*, 253.16: "But Noodynaady's actual ingrate tootle is of come into the garner mauve . . . ." Sayers, *P*, 57: "[A] proper noody-nahdy he is . . . ." Fitzmaurice, *F*, 99: "[I]t could just happen that a noody-nawdy like him would have a mule-fit at the most awkward moment."

not to put a tooth in it (them)   see: tooth in it (them).

nourishment   *n.* alcohol (euph.). Sayers, *P*, 74: "[W]ouldn't a scrap o' sense be better to you than that nourishment!"

Och (Ugh, Ach, Augh)   *excl.* indicates surprise, sorrow or irritation; used at the beginning of a sentence. [Ir. *och (uch)*.] Hyde, *L*, 69: "Ugh, O Una, do you think it a sickly or sorrowful thing / Me to be making melancholy alone?"

ochone (ochanee, och hone, oh hon, oh hone, ohone, achone)   *excl.* alas. [< Ir. *ochón*, alas.] Yeats, *PL*, 32: "Ochone! The treasure-room is broken in." Irvine, *L*, 66: "The light's gone out o' m' home, an' darkness fills 'm heart, Anna, an' it's the sun that'll shine for m' no more! Ochone! Ochone!"

of *prep.* a com. substitution for "on" in references to days of the week. Joyce, *U*, 111: "He died of a Tuesday."

Og (Oge) *a.* young, youthful, junior; com. in names. [< Ir. *óg*.] Lover, *P*, 172: "Above the weirs the silver salmon leap, / While Cormac Oge and I all lonely weep!" Cf. Tir na nOg. ["Eileen Og" is a song; "Eileen Oge" is the name of a boat in *The Big House of Inver* (1925), a novel by E. OE. Somerville and Martin Ross.]

oh hon (oh hone, ohone) see: ochone.

oil *n.* alcohol (sl.). O'Casey, *J*, 105: *"He is a man of forty years of age, ... fond of his 'oil' but determined to conquer the habit before he dies."*

oinseach (oneshuck, one shuck) *n.* a female fool (pej.); occ. male. [Ir. *óinseach*.] Fitzmaurice, *F*, 102: ". . . I can't prevent the oneshuck slipping from me." *Ibid.*, 89: "Disist, one shuck!" See: omadhaun. [The form in the second quot. is probably a misprint; "The oinseach sees the omadhaun's faults" (prov.).]

oireachtas (oireactas) *n.* an assembly, usu. for cultural purposes; the Irish Legislature (since independence). [Ir. *oireachtas*.] Pearse, *P*, 173: "She would be sent to Dublin to sing a song at the Oireachtas." Gregory, *P*, 57: "I was looking the other day through a collection of poems, lately taken down from the Irish-speaking country people for the *Oireactas*, the great yearly meeting of the Gaelic League . . . ." [Oireachtas na Gaeilge is the annual festival of the Gaelic league; An tOireachtas is the Irish Legislature, which consists of two houses, Dail Eireann (lower house) and Seanad Eireann (upper house); *Oireachtas Companion* (5 vols. 1923-45), by William J. Flynn, is a reference work.]

old hen, the *s. phr.* influenza. Synge, *P*, 163: "Would you have him sending down droughts, and fevers, and the old hen and the cholera morbus."

old man *s. phr.* beer slops sold to unsuspecting customers in pubs (sl.). Joyce, *U*, 58: "Coming up redheaded curates from the county Leitrim, rinsing empties and old man in the cellar." See: curate.

old one (ould wan) *s. phr.* an old woman (usu. pej., Dub.). Fitzmaurice, *R*. 62: "[S]he remarked. . . that I was a rale Dublin ould wan — just like Jimmy O'Dea's dames from Kimmage. Did you ever in your life hear anything more insulting than that?" Cf. one (wan).

ollamh (ollav, ollave) *n.* a master of art or science, a learned man a professor, a sage. [Ir. *ollamh*.] Campbell, *P*, 215: "Led by the cone / Of Coemhghen's Tower, proud travellers came, — / Kings . . . And ollamhs, too . . . ." Joyce, *U*, 184: "Glittereyed, his rufous skull close to his green capped desklamp sought the face, bearded amid darkgreener shadow, an ollav, holyeyed." Yeats, *PO*, 17:

"[E] very ancient Ollave said, / While he bent down his fading head, / 'He drives away the northern cold.' "

omadhaun (omadhawn, omadaun, amadan, muddhaun)   *n.* a male fool (pej.); occ. female. [< Ir. *amadán*.] Joyce, *D*, 161. "[T] hey get these thundering big country fellows, omadhauns, you know, to drill." Somerville and Ross, *RME*, 202: "Well, and can't ye put the pilliasse on the floor under it, ye omadhawn?" Fitzmaurice, *R*, 40: "Don't mind that omadaun, Jack." ['The oinseach sees the omadhaun's faults" (prov.); see: oinseach; *The Amadan* is a play by Dion Boucucault; Donal the Fool in *The Enchanted Land*, a play by George Fitzmaurice, introduces himself as Donal the Omadhaun.]

on his keeping   see: keeping, on his

on the jar   see: jar.

on the sthra   see: stravage.

one (wan)   *n.* a female (pej.). Synge *P*, 103: "That one should be right company!" O'Casey, *J*, 85: ". . . I don't blame him for fightin' shy of people like that Joxer fella an' that oul' Madigan wan . . . ." Cf. old one (ould wan).

oolaghaun   see: ullagone.

oro (uroo)   *inter.* oho, yoho (used in choruses). [Ir. *oró*.] Ferguson, *P*, 128: "Then, Oro, come with me! come with me! come with me! / Oro, come with me! brown girl, sweet!" ["Ballinamona Oro" is a song.]

ould wan   see: old one.

Ourselves Alone   see: Sinn Fein.

outside car (outsider, side car)   *n.* a two-wheeled, horse-drawn, open passenger vehicle; the so-called Irish jaunting car. Colum, *PC*, 9: "Owen Paralon brought out / The big-boned mare, and yoked the outside car." Joyce, *D*, 153: "When they came out into Grafton Street Mr Power whistled for an outsider." Gregory, *SP*, 88: "[B] ut for the wheat that was to be sowed there would be more side cars and common cars at my father's funeral . . . than any funeral ever left your own door."

overright (over-right)   *s. phr.* against, in front of, opposite. [Perh. < Ir. *ós-comhair*, over-opposite, confused with *ós-cóir*, over-right.] Fitzmaurice, *R*, 4: "Is it in your senses you are and to be making mention of charges overright Mulcair the smith?" Somerville and Ross, *RME*, 239: "I couldn't tell the words that she said to me . . . and she over-right three crowds o' men that was on the sthrand."

ownshuck   see: oinseach.

P. P.   *abbr.* Parish Priest. Fitzmaurice, *R*, 85: "[T] isn't like the P. P. who can take what's put before him, he did for his three hard-boiled duck eggs indeed at my own station last week. . . ." See: station(s).

paistin see: pastheen.

Pale, the (English pale) *n.* the area around the city of Dublin under effective English jurisdiction, which increased or decreased as English power in Ireland waxed or waned. MacNamara, *V*, 106: "Not one of them had ever been able to fancy the thoughts of Hugh De Lacy as he drew near this noble monument to his glory after some successful expedition against the chieftains of the Pale." [The Norman De Lacy was granted the Kingdom of Meath by King Henry II in 1172. The term English pale appears in literature as early *A View of the Present State of Ireland* (ca. 1596) by Edmund Spenser: "Beyond the Pale" is a poem by Austin Clarke (1896-1961); *Beyond the Pale and Other Stories* (1981) is a collection of short stories by William Trevor (1928-); *Ireland Beyond the Pale* (1986) is a photo essay by Padraig O Flannabhra.]

pampooties *n (pl.).* Aran Island moccasins made from pieces of raw cow-skin. [< Ir. *pampúta*.] Synge, *A*, 65: "[I]t was decided to make me a pair of pampooties, which I have been wearing to-day among the rocks."

parlatic *a.* extremely drunk (sl.). [Var. of paralytic.] Synge, *P*, 143: ". . . I not three weeks with the Limerick girls drinking myself silly and parlatic from the dusk to the dawn."

Parliament whiskey see: poteen.

parliamentary side of your arse, sit (down) on the *c. phr.* shut up (pej.); sit down and be quiet (pej.). Joyce, *U*, 342: "Arrah, sit down on the parliamentary side of your arse for Christ's sake and don't be making a public exhibition of yourself." See: arrah.

pass-remarkable *s. phr.* to be critical or pass unwelcome remarks. O'Casey, *P*, 139: "[Y]ou're not goin' to be pass-remarkable to any lady in my company."

pastheen (paistin) *n.* a little child (end.). [< Ir. *páiste*, child + een, H.E. dim. suf. < Ir. *ín*.] Ferguson, *P*, 128: "Oh, my fair Pastheen is my heart's delight, / Her gay heart laughs in her blue eye bright . . . ." Yeats, *PO*, 325: "My Paistin Finn is my sole desire . . . ." See: een, finn. ["Pasteen Finn" is a poem by Samuel Ferguson; the "tune" of W. B. Yeats's poem, "Two Songs Rewritten for the Tune's Sake", is the traditional "Paistin Finn", which appears in Joyce's *Finnegans Wake* as "pawsdeen fiunn" (95. 17-18).]

pattern (patthern, patteran, patron) *n.* a gathering for religious activities at a place associated with a local patron saint on a feast day. [< patron.] Fitzmaurice, *F*, 11: " 'Twas on a summer's day and we going to the pattern of Lyre. . . ." [Some patterns degenerated into occasions of debauchery, violence and faction fights, and were suppressed; "Pattern of Saint Brendan", a poem by Francis MacManus (1909-1965), depicts such a pattern.]

Paudeen   *n.* a plebeian Irishman (usu. pej.). [< Ir. *Pádraig* (Patrick) + H.E. dim. suf. een, < Ir. *ín.*] Yeats, *PO*, 119: "You gave, but will not give again / Until enough of Paudeen's pence / By Biddy's halfpennies have lain / To be 'some sort of evidence' . . . ." See: een, Biddy. ["Paudeen" is a poem by W. B. Yeats; "A Handsome Lad is Paudeen" is a song.]

pay of the Castle, in the   *c. phr.* an informer (pej.); after Dublin Castle, nerve centre of Br. rule in Ireland. Joyce, *D*, 125: "I believe half of them are in the pay of the Castle." Cf. Castle Catholic, Castle hack, shoneen, West Briton. [The phr. is one of a number of pejorative terms for those who supported, or were suspected of supporting, Br. rule in Ireland.]

pee   see: dee.

peeler   *n.* a member of the (Royal) Irish Constabulary (nic., occ. pej.); after Robert Peel, Secretary for Ireland and founder of the force, 1812-18. Synge, *P*, 61: "[I]f they find his corpse stretched above in the dews of dawn, what'll you say then to the peelers or the Justices of the Peace?" Cf. garda. [Royal was added to name in 1867; it was replaced by the *Gárda Siochána* in 1923; "The Peeler and the Goat" is a very popular satiric song about the force by Jeremiah O'Ryan (d. 1855); "Peelers v Patriots" is chapter of *The Black and Tans* (1959) by Richard Bennett.]

peloothered (peluthered)   *a.* very drunk (sl.). Joyce, *D*, 160: "It happened that you were peloothered, Tom, said Mr Cunningham gravely." Cf. fluthered.

perish (kill) the Danes, that would   see: Danes.

phaties   see: praties.

phillelew   see: allilu.

phuca   see: pooka.

piatez   see: praties.

pillallo (pillelew, pillilew, pilliloo)   see: alilu.

pirtas   see: praties.

pishog (pishogue, pishrogue, pishthroges, spishoge)   *n.* a charm, spell, witchcraft; a superstitious belief or practice. [< Ir. *piseog.*] Joyce. *U*, 321: "A pishogue, if you know what that is." ["Pishogues" (1924) is a short story by Nell Gay; "Old Pishrogues" is a chapter in *Irish Folk Ways* (1957) by E. Estyn Evans.]

plabbery   *a.* soft, sloppy (pej.). [< Ir. *plab*, a soft or foolish person.] Joyce, *U*, 743: "[H]e was . . . making a declaration with his plabbery kind of a manner to her like he did to me . . . ."

Plain of Conn   *met.* Ireland; after Conn Céd Cathach (of the Hundred Battles), founder of the Middle Kingdom (Meath) and the High Kingship of Tara (ca. 200 A.D.). Corkery, *M*, 97: "[T]he myriad love-names of Ireland were invoked . . . — The Little Dark Rose, the Sean Bhean Bhocht, the Silk of the Kine, Innisfail, the Plain of Conn, Fodhla, Banbha . . . ." See: Dark Rosaleen (Little Dark Rose), poor old woman (Sean Bhean Bhocht), silk of the kine, Inisfail (Innisfail), Fodhla, Banba.

plamais (plamaus, plawmaus, plomaus)　*n.*, *v.* soft-talk, flattery. [< Ir. *plámás.*] Fitzmaurice, *F*, 82: "Don't be rising me more, now, with your hypocricies and your plomauses." Joyce, *FW*, 457.30: "[L]isten, I want, girls palmassing, to whisper my whish. . . ." See: whisht (whish).

Plan Kathleen　see: Cathleen (Kathleen) ni Houlihan.

planxty　*n.* a lively Irish (harp) tune. [Perh. < L. *plangere*, to strike, beat.] Joyce, *FW*, 397.05: "And there she was right enough, that lovely sight enough, the girleen bawn asthore, as for days galore, of planxty Gregory." See: een, bawn, asthora (asthore). [There is an obvious allusion to Augusta Gregory in this quotation. "Planxty Connor", "Drury", "Irwin", "Maguire", and "Reynolds" are a few of many such tunes; The Planxties is the name a musical group.]

pledge, the　*n.* the solemn promise to abstain from alcohol made by a member of the Pioneer Total Abstinence Association, a temperance organization founded in 1838 by Father Theobald Mathew (1790-1865) in Cork. Joyce, *D*, 61: "It was no use making him take the pledge: he was sure to break out again in a few days."

pluck 1　*n.* cheek. [< Ir. *pluc.*] Joyce, *U*, 346: "Cissy Caffery bent over him to tease his fat little plucks and the dainty dimple on his chin."

pluck 2　*n.* internal organs of animals used for food. [Engl. pluck.] Irvine, *L*, 52: "In nine cases out of ten, Sunday 'kitchen' was a cow's head, a 'calf's head and pluck', a pair of cow's feet, a few sheep's 'trotters', or a quart of sheep's blood." See: kitchen.

po (poe)　*n.* chamberpot (sl.). [Engl. sl. < Fr. *pot de chambre.*] Joyce, *FW*, 204.12: "[S]he was . . . poing her pee. . . ."

pogue　*v.*, *n.* kiss. [< Ir. *póg.*] Joyce, *U*, 205: "There he keened a wailing rune: — *Pogue mahone! Acushla machree!* It's destroyed we are from this day! It's destroyed we are surely." See: arrah, keen, poguemahone, acushla, machree. [This quot. from Joyce's *Ulysses* is one of a number of parodies in the work of the rendering of Irish folk speech by J. M. Synge and others; Arrah-na-Pogue (of the Kiss) is the heroine of *Arrah-na-Pogue* (1864), a play by Dion Boucicault; "The Pogues" is the name of a rock band.]

poguemahone (pogue mahone, pog-mo-hone)　*c. phr.* kiss my arse (pej.). [< Ir. *póg mo thón.*] Joyce, *U*, 205: "There he keened a wailing rune: — *Pogue mahone! Acushla machree!* It's destroyed we are from this day! It's destroyed we are surely." [This quot. from Joyce's *Ulysses* is one of a number of parodies in the work of the rendering of Irish folk speech by J. M. Synge and others; Poguemahone Hall is an iron. name for "a late Norman foundation," in *Slattery's Sago Saga*, an unfinished novel by Flann O'Brien.]

poirse (poirsin)   *n.* an entry, passage or laneway. [Ir. *póirse* or *póirsín* (dim.).] Corkery, *S*, 128: "A farmer using the *poirse* of a neighbour as a short cut for his turf or corn may suddenly behold . . . the rough effigy of one of the dwellers of the valley . . . ." *Ibid.*, 35: "She would start off before the sun had risen, would pilot the ass and cart down the rough mountainy *poirsin*. . . ."

pole, up the   see: up the pole.

polis (polismen)   *n (pl.).* police. [Rare or obs. Engl. pron. com. in H.E.] Joyce, *U*, 422: "Don't be all night before the polis sees us." O'Casey, *J*, 99: Two polismen below wantin' you."

ponny   *n.* a small tin drinking-vessel. [Perh. an abbr. of pannikin.] Corkery, *M*, 88: "[H]is wife . . . brought in a ponny of milk . . . ."

pooka (pookha, puca, phuca)   *n.* puck, a type of fairy or mischevious and sometimes malignant goblin. [< Ir. *púca*.] Joyce, *FW*, 102.15: "[T]he churchclose clinked . . . with pawns, prelates and pookas . . . ." Campbell, *P*, 144: "The Púca's come again, / Who long has hid away / In cave or twilight glen; Too shy, too proud to play / Under the eye of day." [The pooka generally appears in the form of a horse, but sometimes in the form of another animal, such as a bull or goat, which tries to get its victim on its back and terrify him by galloping furiously across the landscape, before dumping him into some bog or quagmire. ["The Kildare Pooka" is a story by Patrick Kennedy (1801-1873); "The Piper and the Púca" is a story by Douglas Hyde; "The Púca" is a poem by Joseph Campbell; Pooka MacPhellimey is a character in the novel *At Swim-Two-Birds* (1939) by Flann O'Brien; "Horns on the Pooka' is a chapter of *Island Cross-Talk* (1986) by Thomás O'Crohan.]

pooley (pooly)   *n.* urine (sl., Dub.). Joyce, *U*, 541: "It's as limp as a boy of six's doing his pooley behind a cart."

poor old Granuaile   see: Granuaile.

poor old woman (shan van vocht)   *met.* Ireland: one of many code names used when patriotic references to Ireland were proscribed (lit.). [< Ir. *sean bhean bhocht*, poor old woman.] Ledwidge, *B*, 305: "I heard the Poor Old Woman say: / 'At break of day the fowler came, / And took my blackbirds from their songs / Who loved me well thro' shame and blame.' " O'Casey, *P*, 139: ". . . Fluther can remember th' time, an him only a dawny chiselur, bein' taught at his mother's knee to be faithful to the Shan Van Vok!" See:

blackbird, fluthered (Fluther), dawney (dawny), chiseller (chiselur); cf. Cathleen (Kathleen) ni Houlihan, Dark Cow, Dark Rosaleen, Granuaile, four green fields, silk of the kine. ["The Shan Van Vocht" is a traditional patriotic song about the arrival of French support for the insurrection of 1798, and the title of a nationalist literary magazine (1896-1899), edited by Ethna Carbery (1866-1902) and Alice Milligan (1866-1953) in Belfast; *The Shan Van Vocht; Hugh Roach the Ribbonman* (1887) is a novel by James Murphy (1839-1921); Roger Casement (1864-1916) used the Irish form of the name as a pseudonym; The Poor Old Woman is a character in *Cathleen ni Houlihan* (1902), a one-act play by W. B. Yeats, and in *The Bursting of the Bubble* (1903), a one-act comedy by Douglas Hyde; "The Sean Bhean Bhocht" (1957) is a poem by John Montague; the name appears in Joyce's *Finnegans Wake* as "puir old wobban" (13.24).]

poor scholar *n.* an apprentice hedge schoolmaster or aspirant to the priesthood from an impoverished family in the first half of the 19th c. Carleton, *S*, 285: "As to the state of the 'poor scholar,' it exceeded belief; for he was friendless and unprotected." See: hedge school. ["The Poor Scholar" is a story by William Carleton; "A Poor Scholar of the 'Forties" is a poem by Padraic Colum; *Poor Scholar* (1948) is a study of Carleton by Benedict Keily (1919-).]

Pope's nose, the *c. phr.* the tail stump of a fowl (iron.). Joyce, *P*, 32: "There's a tasty bit here we call the pope's nose."

possing *a.* very wet. [< poss, to splash: rare or obs. Engl.] Joyce, *U*, 357: "[W]hen she undid the strap she cried out, holy saint Denis, that he was possing wet and to double the half blanket the other way under him." [There is a pun on the term in Joyce's *Finnegans Wake*: "[T]he possing of the showers . . ." (51.02).]

potato ward *n.* an electoral ward won by bribery. Joyce, *FW*, 240.36-241.01: "Not true what chronicles is bringing his portemanteau priamed full potatowards."

poteen (potheen, potteen) *n.* an illicit whiskey; usu. made in remote parts of the country. [< Ir. *poitín*.] Yeats, *PL*, 103: "Broth of the best, stirabout, poteen, wine itself, he said!" Joyce, *U*, 658: "[W]ith rough and tumble gusto to the accompaniment of large potations of potheen and the usual blarney . . . ." Somerville and Ross, *B*, 284: "A small taste of potteen that he might put to hide from me." ["Potteen, Good Luck to Ye, Dear" is a drinking song by the novelist Charles Lever (1806-1872); "The Poteen Maker" is a short story by Michael McLaverty (b. 1907). Licit whiskey was called Parliament whiskey; the two terms are a reflection of a long tradition of illicit distilling in Ireland.]

praties (pratees, phaties, piatez, piaties, pirtas) *n (pl.).* potatoes.

[< Ir. *prátai.*] Joyce, *FW*, 56.26: "[T]here at the Angel were herberged for him poteen and tea and praties and baccy and wine. . . ." Irvine, *L*, 60: "Wud that be Savage givin' us a bit of groun' next year t' raise pirtas?" See: poteen. ["The Garden Where the Praties Grow," and "Oh! The Praties They Are Small Over Here" are songs.]

priesteen   *n.* a little priest (usu., pej.). [priest + H.E. dim. suf. een (< Ir. *ín*).] Joyce, *U*, 215: "The quaker's pate godlily with a priesteen in booktalk." See: een. [This quot. contains a typical Joycean pun; it is both accurate and pejorative: the priest is Patrick S. Dinneen author of *Foclóir Gaedhilge agus Béarla: An Irish-English Dictionary* (1927), who was a small man.]

puca   see: pooka.

puck   *n., v.* a blow, a punch, esp. a blow from the horns of an animal; the blow given to the ball and to strike the ball in the game of hurley. [< Ir. *poc*, a sharp, sudden blow.] Joyce, *U*, 251: "One puck in the wind from that fellow would knock you into the middle of next week, man." Campbell, *P*, 133: "[F]oolish cubs, d'you see, / Would get a fall / At pucking ball . . . ." See: hurley; cf. pucker.

pucker   *n.* a boxer. [< Ir. *poc*, a sharp, sudden blow.] Joyce, *U*, 250: "He stood looking in at the two puckers stripped to their pelts and putting up their props." Cf. puck.

punt   *n.* a pound: the basic unit of Irish currency. [Ir. *punt*, a pound (money or weight).] Joyce, *FW*, 437.18: "Your Punt's Perfume's only in the hatpinny shop beside the reek of the rawny." See: rawney (rawny).

pus (puss)   *n.* mouth (pej.). [< Ir. *pus.*] Fitzmaurice, *F*, 25: "[T]is little would make me give you that fist right in your grizzled puss." Joyce, *U*, 199: "And we to be there, mavrone, and you to be unbeknownst sending us your conglomerations the way we to have our tongues out a yard long like the drouthy clerics do be fainting for a pussful." See: mavrone, do be. [This quot. from Joyce's *Ulysses* is one of a number of parodies in the work of the rendering of Irish folk speech by J. M. Synge and others.]

Put a beggar on horseback   see: beggar on horseback.

put no tooth in it (them)   see: tooth in it (them).

quality (quol'ty), the   *n.* the Ascendancy, the upper class of society. Joyce, *D*, 207: "One fine day the old gentleman thought he'd like to drive out with the quality to a military review in the park." See: Ascendancy.

quare   *a.* strange, odd, peculiar, memorable, queer. [18th c. Engl. pron. of queer, com. in H.E.] Joyce, *FW*, 215.13: "[S]ure he was the quare old buntz too, Dear Dirty Dumpling, foostherfather of fingalls and dotthergills." See: footer (foosther). ["The Quare Gander" is a story by Joseph Sheridan Le Fanu (1814-1873); *The Quare Fellow* (1956) is a play by Brendan Behan, and "Yes, quare times" is an article in his *Hold your hour and have another* (1963); *In Dublin's Quare City* is a play by Basil Payne (1928-).]

quol'ty, the   see: quality, the

ra, a'   see: agra.

rack (rack-rent)   *v., n.* to rent land at such excessive rates to tenant farmers that they were reduced to a mere subsistence living. Moore, *M*, 248: "[T]he two were then conjointly to rack-rent poor Murphy. . . ." [Though not exclusive to Ireland, rack-rent was a particularly widespread problem, because of the common practice of absentee Anglo-Irish landlords employing agents to collect rents on their estates in the 18th and 19th c., and is reflected in the title of the first A.I. novel, *Castle Rackrent* (1800) by Maria Edgeworth. The practice is one of a number of abuses explained and condemned by Edmund Spenser in *A View of the Present State of Ireland* (ca. 1596): "landlords there use most shamefully to rack their tenants . . ." (81).]

ragal, a'   see: agra and gal.

raimeis (ramaish, rameish, rawmaish, rawmaysh, rhamaush, raumeis)   *n.* nonsense. [Ir. *raiméis*, romance, nonsense.] Joyce, *U*, 326: "*Raimeis*, says the citizen." Fitzmaurice, *R*, 23: "There is no good in starting a game of hambug and raumeis with her likes. . . ."

raise the wind   *s. phr.* to obtain money by some means or other. Joyce, *U*, 147: "With a heart and a half if I could raise the wind anyhow." [*Raising the Wind* (1803) is a farce by James Kenny (ca. 1780-1849); "RAISING THE WIND" is a heading in the "Aeolus" episode of Joyce's *Ulysses*.]

ramaish (rameish)   see: raimeis.

rambling house   *s. phr.* a house in which people gather in the evenings to gossip, play cards, etc. Sayers, *P*, 14: "At that time Séamus Boland's was generally the 'rambling house': the adults would be playing cards on the table and the youngsters would be in the corner carrying on children's games."

rann   *n.* an Irish quatrain. [Ir. *rann*.] Yeats, *PO*, 56: "*Know, that I would accounted be / True brother of a company / That sang, to sweeten Ireland's wrong, / Ballad and story, rann and song. . . .*" Campbell, *P*, 216: "Low-droned ranns / Mingle, with vivid nearby talk . . . ." [The first two lines (*seoladh*) give the drift of a rann, the second two (*cómhad*) conclude, as in the following, translated by Douglas Hyde: "If yon fat friar be a poor friar / Then a fat desire is his life's rule; / But if man by fat to heaven may aspire, / Then a lean friar is a lean fool." *Ranns and Ballads* (1918) is a volume of verse by Seumas O'Kelly; *Rann* (1948-54) is an Ulster literary periodical edited by Roy McFadden and Barbara Edwards; "The Rann of the Little Playmate" and "A Rann I Made" are poems by Patrick Pearse; "A Rann of Exile" is a poem by Padraic Colum.]

rapparee   *n*. a rebel, a hero, an outlaw (hist., lit.); orig. one of many Irish Catholic landlords who turned to plunder for survival and revenge following their dispossession by Cromwell. [< Ir. *ropaire*.] Joyce, *U*, 295: "Doing the rapparee and Rory of the hill." See: Rory of the hill. ["The Raparee" is a chapter in *The O'Briens and the O'Flahertys* (1827), a novel by Lady Morgan (ca. 1776-1859); *Redmond, Count O'Hanlon, the Irish Rapparee* (1862) is a novel by William Carleton; *The Rapparee* is a play by Dion Boucicault; "Rapparees" is a poem by Richard Murphy (1927-).]

rawmaish   see: raimeis.

rawney (rawny)   *n*. a sickly person or animal. [< Ir. *ránaidhe*.] Joyce, *FW*, 437.18: "Your Punt's Perfume's only in the hatpinny shop beside the reek of the rawny." See: punt, reek.

rawsie   see: rossy.

red martyrdom   see: martyrdom, red (white)

red rex   *n*. a penny or halfpenny (sl.); from the copper colour and king's head on such British coins. [L. *rex*, king.] O'Casey, *J*, 86: "Not as much as a red rex, man . . . ." [The Irish Free State penny, introduced in 1928 (W. B. Yeats was chairman of the coinage committee), replaced the king's head with the Irish harp, even though the king was still, officially, head of state.]

ree-raw (reeraw)   *n*. fuss, confusion, clamour, revelry. [< Ir. *rí-rá*.] O'Casey, *T*, 96: "This Tosthal ree-raw is makin' youse all too randy." See: Tostal (Tosthal). [In Joyce's *Finnegans Wake*, the term is converted into a chant: "[T]rying with pious clamour to heedle Tipperaw raw raw reeraw puteters out of Now Sealand . . ." (111.01).]

reek   *n*. a stack of hay, straw, corn, or turf; a mountain. [Var. of rick.] Pearse, *P*, 304: "[T]hey looking on grassy parks, and on green-topped woods, and on high-headed reeks . . . ." Colum, *PC*, 86: "[T]he weavers' bundles are carried in his creels on asses' backs / Across the Reeks . . . ." [MacGillicuddy's Reeks in Co. Kerry contain Ireland's highest peak, Carrauntoohil (3,485 ft.).]

refooting (refutting)   see: foot.

Reilly, the life of   see: life of Reilly.

relic   *n*. penis (sl., iron.). Campbell, *P*, 258: "Twas in the town of Ballnaskellick / He rubbed her trouble with his relic." ["A touch (rub) of the relic" is a com. irreverent euph. for sexual intercourse.]

return room   *n.* a room in an extension at the back of a house, projecting into the yard at a right angle to the line of the building: a com. feature of Dublin's tenements. Joyce, *U*, 302: "[T]he other boot which he had been looking for was at present under the commode in the return room. . . ." [The setting of Sean O'Casey's play, *The Shadow of a Gunman*, is a return room of a tenement.]

rex   see: red rex.

rhamaush   see: raimeis.

Riley, the life of   see: life of Reilly.

rinnce fada (rinka-fadha)   *n.* a traditional dance in jig time, said to resemble the continental La Rinka. [Ir. *rinnce fada*, long dance.] Corkery, *H*, 99: "We would laugh, we would cycle, we would dance the rinnce fada in the farm kitchens . . . ."

roe   see: ruadh.

Róisín Dubh (Dhu, Duhv)   see: Dark Rosaleen.

roo   see: rua.

roon   see: aroon.

Rory of the Hill   *c. phr.* a rebel; from the title of a song by Charles J. Kickham (1828-1882). Joyce, *U*, 295: "Doing the rapparee and Rory of the hill." See: rapparee.

Rosaleen, Dark   See: Dark Rosaleen.

rosiner (rosner, rossiner, roziner, rozziner)   *n.* the first drink of a session, a stiff drink; from the practice of putting rosin on a bow before playing a stringed instrument. Becket, *M*, 86: " 'And the rosiner. . . , will you have that in the lav too?' / Reader, a rosiner is a drop of the hard." ["*A Rosner*: A Woman of No Standing" is a section of *Brendan Behan's Island* (1962).]

ross   *n.* a point, a headland, a promontory; com. in place names. [< Ir. *ros*.] Pearse, *P*, Ap. v: "I see before my eyes . . . a narrow, moaning bay stretching in from the sea on each side of a 'ross;' the 'ross' rising up from the round of the bay . . . ." Yeats, *PO*, 20: "Where the wave of moonlight glosses / The dim grey sands with light, / Far off by furthest Rosses / We foot it all the night . . . ." ["By the Short Cut to the Rosses" is a song by Nora Hopper (1871-1906); *The Rosses* (1918) is a collection of poems by Seamus O'Sullivan (1879-1958).]

rossy (rossie, rawsie)   *n.* a brazen female (pej.). [< Ir. *rásach*.] Joyce, *U*, 365: "If they could run like rossies she could sit so she said . . . ."

roziner (rozziner)   see: rosiner.

rua (ruadh, ruadht, rue, roe, roo)   *a.* red-haired: com. in names. [< Ir. *ruadh*.] Somerville and Ross, *RME*, 244: "[I]t was . . . the home of one Shemus Ruadth, a singer and poet . . . ." [Anne Chute, the Colleen Ruadh, is a character in *The Colleen Bawn* (1860), a melodrama by Dion Boucicault; Darby Ruadh is a character in *Knocknagow* (1879), a novel by Charles Kickham (1828-1882); "Aodh Ruadh O'Domhnaill" (Red Hugh O'Donnell, 1571-1602, Uls. Chieftain) is a poem by Thomas MacGreevy (1893-1967); "The Colleen Rue" is a folksong; Owen Roe O'Neill was a 17th c. Uls. military leader.]

rub of the relic   see: relic.

rue   see: rua.

ruin, a   see: aroon.

said by   see: be said by.

sainted isle   see: Island of Saints and Sages.

Samhain (Saimhuin)   *n.* all hallowtide, the pre-Christian and Christian feast of the dead at the end of October and the beginning of November. [Ir. *Samhain*.] Synge, *R*, 25: "I'll have no call now to be going down and getting Holy Water in the dark nights after Samhain. . . ." ["Samhain" is a poem by J. M. Synge, and a theatre magazine (1901-06, 08) in which W. B. Yeats published a series of essays; "An Samhain" is a poem by Joseph Campbell; "Samhain" is a short story by Dorothy MacArdle (1899-1958); sowans is a form of gruel made and eaten at halloween.]

sarra   see: sorra.

Sassenach (Sassanach)   *n.* an Englishman; the English (pej.). [< Ir. *Sasanach*.] Joyce, *U*, 9: "The Sassenach wants his morning rashers." Gregory, *P*, 232: "[Y]e shall gain the day in every quarter from the Sassanach . . . ." [In Ir. the term can also mean a Protestant, because the vast majority of the English in Ireland after the Reformation were such.]

savourneen   see: mavourneen.

scivvie (skivvie)   *n.* a servant girl (sl., pej.). [Engl. sl.] Joyce, *U*, 322: "Swindled them all, skivvies and badhachs from the county Meath. . . ." See: badhach.

scolog (scullog, scullogue)   *n.* a small farmer, a rustic. [Ir. *scológ*.] Joyce, *FW*, 398.03: "[S]cullogues, churls and vassals . . . ."

sconce   *v.* to look. [Engl. sconce, a lantern or candlestick with a screen and handle or bracket.] Corkery, *S*, 93: " 'Twould be the best of your play to go and have a sconce at it . . . ."

scooge   see: scrooge.

scrah   see: scraw.

scran   see: bad scran.

scraping of the pot (skillet), the   *c. phr.* a woman's last child. [< Ir. *dríodar an chruiscín*.] O'Crohan, *IM*, 1: "I am 'the scrapings of

the pot', the last of the litter." Sayers, *P*, 169: "Often it's 'the scraping of the skillet' is the one you'd like the most." Cf. shake of the
bag. [The act of confessing is jocularly called "scraping the pot."]

scraw (scrah)   *n.* a grassy sod; the top grassy layer of a bog, occ.
used as roofing material. [< Ir. *scraith*.] Moore, *M*, 104: "Begad,
we'd make him wear the grane in raal earnest, and, a foine scraw
it would be. . . ." Corkery, *M*, 75: "[W]hile this storm was gathering above his weed-tattered roof of scrahs, the power of song was
already surging up within him . . . ."

screw   *n.* a job, an income, wages (sl., Dub.). [Engl. sl.] Joyce,
D, 65: "She knew he had a good screw for one thing and she
suspected he had a bit of stuff put by."

screwed   *a.* drunk (sl.). [Engl. sl.] Somerville and Ross, *S*, 50: "[I]t
was market day, and I evaded with difficulty the sinuous course of
carts full of soddenly screwed people."

scrooge (scroodge, scrouge, scooge)   *v.* to crowd, crush or squeeze
in. [Engl. sl.] O'Casey, *H*, 35: "[I]f you can manage to scooge in
don't forget to come up where I'll be sittin'."

scullog (scullogue)   see: scolog.

scunner (skunner)   *v., n.* strong dislike, loathing (Uls.). [Sc.]
Joyce, *FW*, 205.21: "[E]ven the snee that snowdon his hoaring hair
had a skunner against him."

scut   *n.* a contemptible person (pej.). [Perh. < scut, the short tail
of a hare or rabbit.] Fitzmaurice, *F*, 102: "[T]he Mananaan squad
come along . . . chastising the scut for her gumption of thinking
herself a match for the Queen. . . ."

scutter (skitter)   *excl., n.* diarrhoea. Joyce, *U*, 4: "Scutter, he cried
thickly."

Seagan Buidhe   see: Shane Bwee.

seanachie (seanachy, seanchai, seanchaidhe)   see: shanachie.

Seanad [Eireann]   *n.* senate; the upper chamber of An tOireachtas,
the Irish Legislature, which consists of two houses (Dail Eireann is
the lower house). [< Ir. *seanadh*, synod, senate.] Joyce, *FW*, 372.11:
"[T]he snug saloon seanad of our Café Béranger."

segocia (segotcha, skeowsha)   *n.* darling. Joyce, *FW*, 215:12: "Ah,
but she was the queer old skeowsha anyhow, Anna Livia, trinket-
toes!"

senachie (sennachie)   see: shanachie.

'Sha   see: musha.

shake (shakings) of the bag, the   *c. phr.* a woman's last child.
O'Casey, *A*, I, 5: "This had been the shake of the bag, and she knew
she would never have another child." Cf. scrapings of the pot.

shalwn loth   see: slan leat.

shan van vocht   see: poor old woman.
shanachie (shanachee, seanachie, seanchai, seanchaidhe, senachie, sennachie)   *n.* a traditional storyteller. [< Ir. *seanchaidhe.*] O'Kelly, *H*, 179: "Blame not the shanachie, for the shanachie took the people of Kilbeg as he found them, the good and the bad. . . ." Corkery, *S*, 198: "[A]s a seanchaidhe, or storyteller, he had never met his match . . . ." Yeats, *PO*, 435: "And I gazed on the bell-branch, sleep's forebear, far sung by the Sennachies." ["Tom Gressiey, the Irish Senachie" is a short story by William Carleton; *The Shanachie*, which appeared in 1906-07, is a short-lived literary magazine, edited by Joseph Maunsel Hone (1882-1959), to which W. B. Yeats, G. B. Shaw, J. M. Synge and Lady Gregory contributed.]
shanderadan   *n.* an old, rickety carriage (pej.). [Var. of shandrydan.] Joyce, *U*, 448: "[C]oming home along by Foxrock in that old fiveseater shanderadan of a waggonette . . . ."
Shane Bwee (Seagan Buidhe, Yellow John, Yellow George, George)   *n.* John Bull, the English, a loyalist (pej.). [< Ir. *Seán Buidhe*, Yellow (Dirty) John (Bull); and St. George, d. ca. A.D. 303, patron saint of England.] Mangan, *P*, 52: "Yea, even our Princes . . . themselves must bow / Low before the vile Shane Bwee!" Gregory, *P*, 59: " '[T]hey are not satisfied without giving some lines on Seagan Buidhe' (one of the names for England)." Joyce, *U*, 326: "What do the yellowjohns of Anglia owe us for our ruined trade and our ruined hearths?" Sayers, *P*, 96: "*One quiet pleasant morning / As on my couch I slept / Yellow George and his minions / Surrounded me like theft . . . .*" Gregory, *P*, 59: "George will be sent back over the sea . . . ."
shaughran (shaughraun, shoughraun)   *v.* to wander about, out of employment. [< Ir. *seachrán.*] Joyce, *U*, 135: "We'll paralyse Europe as Ignatius Gallaher used to say when he was on the shaughraun." [Conn, the Shaughraun, is the comic rogue-hero of *The Shaughraun* (1874) a play by Dion Boucicault; Shawn Kilshaughraun is a character in *Faustus Kelly* (1943), a play by Myles na gCopaleen (Flann O'Brien).]
shawl (shawlie, shawly)   *n.* a lower-class woman, a female streetvendor; from the large shawls they wear (pej.). Joyce, *U*, 314: "Blind to the world up in a shebeen in Bride street after closing time, fornicating with two shawls and a bully on guard, drinking porter out of teacups." Beckett, *M*, 48: "[T]he solitary shawly like a cloud of latter rain in a waste of poets and politicians . . . ." See: shebeen.
shebeen (shibbeen, shebean-house)   *n.* an illicit drinking establishment; occ. a low-class pub (pej.). [< Ir. *síbín.*] Somerville and Ross, *RME*, 253: "[M]y brother-in-law and I had been taken red-handed

in a 'shebeen', that is to say, a house in which drink is illicitly sold without a license." ["The Shebeen" is a chapter in *Luttrell of Arran* (1865), a novel by Charles Lever (1806-1872).]

shee (sidh, sidhe, sidheog, sheeog)   *n.* a fairy; fairies (lit.). [< Ir. *sídhe*, or *sidheóg*.] Synge, *S*, 229: "Adieu sweet Aengus, Maeve and Fand, / Ye plumed yet skinny Shee, / That poets played with hand and hand / To learn their ecstacy." Campbell, *P*, 184: "From glens come they, / Out of caves and *sidh*-mounds, / And the dead hollows of the hills." *Ibid.*, 33: "It shall not be the battle / Between the folk and the Sidhe / At the rape of a bride from her bed / Or a babe from its mother's knee." Hyde, *S*, 194: "The queen's sheeogs are after me again." ["The Passing of the Shee" is a poem by J. M. Synge; "A Call of the Sidhe" is a poem by A.E. (George Russell); "The Hosting of the Sidhe" is a poem by W. B. Yeats; *The Tinker and the Sheeog* (1902) is a one-act play by Douglas Hyde.]

shibbeen   see: shebeen.

Shinner   *nic.* used by Loyalists and Br. troops for a member or supporter of Sinn Fein or the Irish Republican Army during the War of Independence, 1918-22 (pej.). O'Casey, *P*, 168: "Bessie Burgess is no Shinner, an' never had no thruck with anything spotted be th' fingers o' th' Fenians. . . ." See: Sinn Fein, Fenian; cf. Sinn Feiner.

shite (shyte)   *n.* excrement. [Var. of shit, usu. in. H.E.] Joyce, *U*, 314: "Told him if he didn't patch up the pot, Jesus, he'd kick the shite out of him."

shoneen   *n.* a would-be gentleman; one who attempts to improve his social status by rejecting his Irish heritage and aping English ways (pej.). [< Ir. *Seoinín*, little John (Bull).] Joyce, *D*, 121: "Hasn't the working-man as good a right to be in the Corporation as anyone else — ay, and a better right than those shoneens that are always hat in hand before any fellow with a handle to his name?"

shooler (shuiler, shular, shuler)   *n.* a wanderer, a vagrant, a beggar. [< Ir. *siubhlóir.*] Pearse, *P*, 32: "I was the poorest *shuiler* on the roads of Ireland . . . ." Campbell, *P*, 73: "Then when the shuiler begs, / Be neither hard nor cold; / The share that goes for Christ / Will come a hundred-fold." ["Trip with the Roving Shooler" is a tune; *Shuilers from Healthy Hills* (1893) is the first book of Seumas MacManus (ca. 1868-1960); *The Shuiler's Child* (1909) is a play by Seamus O'Kelly; "What the Shuiler said as she lay by the Fire in the Farmer's House" is a poem by Padraic Colum; "Every Shuiler is Christ" is a poem by Joseph Campbell; the term appears in Joyce's *Finnegans Wake* as "shoolerim" (112.07).]

short twelve   *s. phr.* a shortened form of the Latin Mass conducted at noon on Sunday, which was very popular among those who celebrated on Saturday night. Joyce, *D*, 64: "It was seventeen minutes past eleven: she would have lots of time to have the matter out with Mr Doran and then catch short twelve at Marlborough Street." [The short twelve conducted at the Pro-Cathedral in Marlborough Street, Dublin, was something of an institution. Members of the congregation were known to use stop-watches to select the fastest celebrant, who was given an appropriate nickname. Betting on the results was not unknown.]

shoughraun   see: shaughran.

shraft   *n*. shrovetide. [< shraftyde, an obs. form of shrovetide.] Somerville and Ross, *RME* 239: "Can you deny that you made a proposal of marriage to Con Brickley's daughter last Shraft?" ["The Last Day of Shraft" is an *Irish R.M.* story by E. Œ. Somerville and Martin Ross.]

shraums   *n*. rheumy matter discharged from the eyes. [< Ir. *sream*.] Joyce, *U*, 245: "[H]e wiped away the heavy shraums that clogged his eyes to hear aright."

shuiler (shular, shuler)   see: shooler.

shyte   see: shite.

siabhra   *n*. a phantom, a fairy, a goblin (lit.). [Ir. *siabhra*.] Campbell, *P*, 251: "No hand / But a Siabhra's hand / Out of a dim land / Should pick / These berries . . . ."

side car   see: outside car.

sidh (sidhe, sidheog, sheeog)   see: shee.

signs on (on it)   *s. phr.* used to express proof or consequence of any fact or situation. [Perh. < Ir. *tá an rian air*, he bears signs of it.] O'Casey *J*, 75: ". . . I remember sayin' . . . that the new arrival. . . ud grow up a hardy chiselur if it lived, an' that she'd be somethin' one o' these days that nobody suspected, an' so signs on it, here she is today, goin' to be married to a young man lookin' as if he'd be fit to commensurate in any position in life it ud please God to call him!" See: chiseller (chiselur).

silk of the kine   *met.* Ireland: one of many code names used when patriotic references to Ireland were proscribed (lit.). [< Ir. *síoda na mbó*.] Joyce, *U*, 14: "Silk of the kine and poor old woman, names given to her in old times." See: poor old woman; cf. Cathleen (Kathleen) ni Houlihan, Dark Cow, Dark Rosaleen, four green fields, Granuaile.

silly   *a*. applied to one whose soul has been stolen by the fairies. Yeats, *M*, 88: "[H]e who sleeps here may wake up 'silly', the Sidhe having carried off his soul." See: shee (sidhe); cf. away. [Occ. applied to an elderly person subject to fainting or dizzy spells.]

sing that if you had an air to it, You could   see: You could sing that if you had an air to it.

Sinn Fein (Amhain)   *c. phr., n.* We Ourselves (Alone). [< Ir. *Sinn Féin (Amháin)*.] Joyce, *U*, 335: "[W]hen I got back they were at it dingdong, John Wyse saying it was Bloom gave the idea for Sinn Fein to Griffith to put in his paper all kinds of jerrymandering, packed juries and swindling the taxes off of the Government and appointing consuls all over the world to walk about selling Irish industries." O'Casey, *S*, 20: "Sinn Fein Amhain: him an' him only, Minnie, I seen him with me own two eyes . . . ." [Sinn Fein is the name of a political party inspired by the articles of Arthur Griffith (1871-1922) in the *United Irishman* newspaper (founded in 1899 and from 1906 to 1914 called *Sinn Féin*) in which he advocated passive resistance to British rule, boycott of British products, revival of Irish industries and "government by the King, Lords and Commons of Ireland." It is now the name of the political wing of the Irish Republican Army. *Ourselves Alone* (1959) is a biography of Griffith by Padraic Colum. As the first quot. above indicates, in Joyce's *Ulysses* it is alleged that Griffith got his ideas from Leopold Bloom; Joyce thus makes his fictional character an influential figure in the the creation of modern Ireland. "Ourselves Alone" is a poem published in 1843 in *The Nation* by Sliabh Cuilinn (John O'Hagan, 1822-1890).]

Sinn Feiner   *nic.* used by Loyalists and Br. troops for a member or supporter of Sinn Fein or the Irish Republican Army during the War of Independence, 1918-22 (pej.). Fitzmaurice, *R*, 146: "[W]hat nice things he said in his letter about the downfall of a good old Anglo-Irish family, our beautiful residence burnt down by the Sinn Feiners. . . ." See: Sinn Fein; cf. Shinner.

sit down on the parliamentary side of your arse   see: parliamentary side of your arse, sit (down) on.

skeezing   *v.* peeping (sl.). Joyce, *U*, 303: "Old Garryowen started growling again at Bloom that was skeezing around the door."

skeogh (skeough)   see: skib.

skeowsha   see: segotcha.

skib (skip, skeogh, skeough, skihogue, skillogue)   *n.* a shallow wicker basket for potatoes. [< Ir. *sciobóg*.] Colum, *PO*, 85: "[T]he skib, / In which potatoes from the pot are poured . . . ." Gregory, *P*, 109: "Then the potatoes were ready, and they were put on a skip for dinner . . . ."

skitter   see: scutter.

skiver   *v., n.* skewer. [Obs. form of skewer com. in H.E.] Gregory, *P*, 57: "[T] hey were glad when they saw those that had put them out put out themselves, and every one of them skivered."

skivvie   see: scivvie.

skunner   see: scunner.

sky farmer   *n.* a small hill-side farmer, a farmer without land. Corkery, *S*, 19: ". . . Chrissie Collins was a farmer's daughter, a small hill-side farmer, a 'sky' farmer." Cf. hillsider.

slainte   *sal.* health: a com. Ir. and H.E. toast. [Ir. *sláinte*.] Beckett, *M*, 148: "To Hymen's gracious mussy and protection we commit them, now, henceforth and for evermore. Slainte."

slan leat (slan leath, slawn lath, shalwn loth)   *sal.* safe with you: a com. Ir. and H.E. farewell, said esp. to one departing. [Ir. *slán leat*.] Joyce, *U*, 314: "*Slan leat*, says he." *Ibid.*, 436: "BLOOM: Haha, *Merci.* Esperanto. *Slan leath*." [Not normally used as a drinking toast, as it is in the first quot. from Joyce's *Ulysses*.]

slane (slean, sleaghan)   *n.* a narrow spade used for cutting turf (a wing set at right angles to the blade allows a complete sod to be cut with a single stroke); a measure of turf cut by a turf-cutting team. [< Ir. *sleaghán*.] Campbell, *P*, 147: "Coasters. . . know the feel of oars better than slanes and rakes. . . ."

slawn lath   see: slan leat.

slean   see: slane.

sleeveen (sleeven, sleiveen, slieveen)   *n.* a smooth-talking, sly, untrustworthy person (pej.). [Ir. *slighbhín*.] Colum, *PO*, 126: "Tomorrow, Mavourneen, a sleeven weds . . . ." Yeats, *PO*, 24: "In trust he took John's lands; / Sleiveens were all his race; / And he gave them as dowers to his daughters, / And they married beyond their place." Campbell, *P*, 216: "Mountain folk / The elect of Fate, thuswise became / Repositories of fine gold, — / Tradition's homing: poor slieveens, / Tillers of rundale, fishers, herds, / Whom, though (sad wretches) scant in much, / In much were full." See: een, mavourneen. [Joseph Campbell's use of this com. term in a non-pej. sense is most unusual.]

slewder (slewsther, sloother)   *v.* to coax, to wheedle, to flatter (pej.). [< Ir. *slusaire*, a dissembler, a wheedler.] Joyce, *U*, 771: "[H] e used to amuse me the things he said with the half sloothering smile on him. . . ."

slieveen   see: sleeveen.

sliotar   see: hurley.

sloother   see: slewder.

sluig   *n.* a quagmire. [Perh. < Ir. *slogaide*, a quagmire.] Synge, *S*, 41: "[T] here's a small path only, and it running up between two sluigs where an ass and cart would be drowned."

smahan   *n.* a taste, a small quantity, especially of drink. [< Ir.

smeachán.] Joyce, *D*, 96: "We'll just have just one little smahan more and then we'll be off."

smather (smaather) *v.*, *n.* to break in pieces, to beat; a heavy blow. [< Ir. *smeádar*, a heavy blow.] Joyce, *U*, 770: "[W]hat a question if I smathered it all over his wrinkly old face for him. . . ."

smug *v.* to kiss; to toy amorously in secret. [Engl. dial.] Joyce, *P*, 42: "What did that mean about the smugging in the square?" [This term appears in A.I. literature as early the late 17th c. ms. *Purgatorium Hibernicum.*]

snug *n.* a small, comfortable, semi-private room in an old fashioned pub. [Engl.] Joyce, *D*, 89: "He put his penny on the counter and, leaving the curate to grope for it in the gloom, retreated out of the snug as furtively as he had entered it." See: curate.

Soft day (morning) *s. phr.*, *sal.* a mild, wet day. [< Ir. *lá (maidin) bog.*] Joyce, *U*, 31: "Soft day, sir John." Joyce, *FW*, 619.20: "Soft morning, city!" ["A Soft Day" is a poem by Winnifred M. Letts (1882-1972); *Soft Day* (1980) is a miscellany of contemporary Irish writing ed. Peter Fallon and Sean Golden.]

soggart (sogarth, soggarth) *n.* a priest (end.). [< Ir. *sagart.*] O'Casey, *J*, 69: "Who was it led the van, Soggart Aroon? / Since the fight first began, Soggart Aroon?" Joyce, *U*, 296: "From his girdle hung a row of seastones . . . and on these were graven with rude yet striking art the tribal images of many Irish heroes and heroines of antiquity, Cuchulin . . . Soggarth Eoghan O'Growney . . . Christopher Columbus . . . The Man in the Gap . . . Dark Rosaleen . . . ." See: aroon, man in the gap, Dark Rosaleen. [As the O'Casey quot. suggests, "Soggarth Aroon" is a popular patriotic song, by the novelist John Banim (1798-1842); *Shawn the Soggarth, the Priest Hunter* is a novel by Matthew Archdeacon (ca. 1800-1863); *The Soggarth Aroon* (1907) is a popular novel by Joseph Guinan (ca. 1870- ?).]

soogaun see: sugan.

sop *n.* a wisp of hay or straw used to stop a hole; a slight or insigificant person. [Ir. *sop.*] Fitzmaurice, *F*, 21: "[H]e can't renayge himself to put a sop in the thatch. . . ." Corkery, *M*, 130: "[S]he steals up the lane outside, a poor rag of a woman, a poor sop off the roads, not knowing what was before her . . . ."

sorra (sorrow, sarra) *ad.* not (emph.). [A euph. for devil.] O'Casey, *J*, 65: "Sorra many'll go into mournin' for him."

sorry for your trouble(s), I am *s. phr.*, *sal.* used to greet one who has been bereaved. Corkery *S*, 152: "He twisted the horse about with a strong wrist, touched his cap, and said: 'I'm sorry for your trouble, sir.'"

soulth (sowlth) *n.* a ghost, an apparition. [< Ir. *samhailt.*] Joyce, *U*, 412. "Tare and ages, what way would I be resting at all, he muttered thickly, and I tramping Dublin this while back with my share of songs and himself after me the like of a soulth or a bullawurrus?" See: tare (tare and ages), himself, bullawurrus. [The quot. from *Ulysses* is one of a number of parodies in the work of the rendering of Irish folk speech by J. M. Synge and others.]

soup, take   *v.* to become a Protestant. See: souper.

souper (soupir)   *n.* a Protestant, a Protestant missionary (pej.); from the practice by some Protestant of combining proselytizing and food distribution in times of famine. Gregory, *SP*, 41: "Sure you don't think he'd turn souper and marry her in a Protestant church?" Sayers, *P*, 44: "He went very hard against the 'soupers' who were plentiful in the locality in those days." Cf. bird's nest, take soup, Swaddler, boiled Protestants. [Souper was originally a pej. term for a Catholic who became a Protestant in return for food. Leopold Bloom in Joyce's *Ulysses* recalls its origin: "They say they used to give pauper children soup to become protestants in the time of the potato blight" (180); *Souperism: Myth or Reality* (1970), by D. Bowen, is a study of the practice, which was opposed by some Protestants and bitterly resented by most Catholics.]

southron   *n.* a native of the south. [Sc. and N. Engl. dial. var. of southern.] Corkery, *H*, 13: " 'Do you wish it? Do you wish it?' he blurted out, in the quick way of the southron."

sowans (sowens)   see: Samhain.

spailpin (spalpeen, spawleen)   *n.* an itinerant farm labourer (not necessarily landless); a rascal (pej.). [Ir. *spailpín*.] Gregory, *SP*, 224: "[H]e was standing, a *spailpin* with his spade in his hand, seeking work at the Easter fair." Joyce, *FW*, 32.16: "[T]he hungerlean spalpeens of Lucalizod. . . ." [The term appears in A.I. literature as early as Jonathan Swift's *A Dialogue in Hibernian Style* (1735); *An Spalpín Fánach* is a well-known, anon. poem in Ir.; "The Spalpeen's Complaint of the Cranbally Farmer" is a song.]

spake   *n.* a speech, saying, sermon or opinion. [18th c. Engl. pron. of speak.] Joyce, *FW*, 338.23: ". . . Malorazzias spikes her, coining a speak a spake!" Friel, *T*, 388: "[T]here was a spake I used to have off by heart."

spaug (spawg)   *n.* a big, clumsy foot or hand (pej.). [< Ir. *spág*, leg, foot, paw (usu. pej.).] Joyce, *U*, 129: "Taking off his flat spaugs and the walk."

spawleen   see: spailpin.

spishoge   see: pishog.

spoiled nun (priest)   *n.* a postulant or student-priest who does not to continue in clerical life. Joyce, *P*, 35: "[H]e had heard his father say that she was a spoiled nun and that she had come out of the convent in the Alleghanies when her brother had got the money from the savages for the trinkets and the chainies." See: chanies. [Until recently, such a person was considered a social disgrace, was often disowned by family and friends, and forced to emigrate.]

squaddy   see: swaddy.

squireen (half-sir, half-mounted man / gentleman)   *n.* an individual on the lower fringes of the the the gentry, particularly one who aped the ways of Ascendancy (usu. pej.). [< squire + H.E. dim. suf. een. (< Ir. *ín*).] Boucicault, *C*, 53: "Genus, squireen — a half sir, and a whole scoundrel." Yeats, *PO*, 221: "Come old, necessitous, half-mounted man. . . ." See: een, Ascendancy. [*The Squireen* (1903) is a novel by Shan F. Bullock (1865-1935); "The Half-Sir" (1829) is a story by Gerald Griffin; Edith Somerville considered Flurry Knox, of the *Irish R. M.* stories, to be a half-sir. The contempt the squireen generated is suggested by P. W. Joyce's remark: 'The class of squireen is nearly extinct: 'Joy be with them' " (*ESI.*, 333).]

stag (stagg)   *n.* an informer, a traitor (sl.). [Engl. sl.] Pearse, *P*, 21: "Is it a boy with that gesture of the head, that proud, laughing gesture, to be a coward or a stag?"

staggeen   *n.* a worn-out, worthless old horse. [stag + een, H.E. dim. suf. een (< Ir. *ín*.).] Somerville and Ross, *RM*, 113: "[I]s it that little staggeen from the mountains; sure she's somethin' about the same age with meself. . . ."

stare   *n.* a starling. [Engl. dial.] Synge, *PO*, 48: "Thrush, linnet, stare and wren, / Brown lark beside the sun, / Take thought of kestril, sparrow-hawk, / Birdlime, and roving gun." ["The Stare's Nest by My Window" is a poem by W. B. Yeats.]

Stater (Free Stater)   *n.* a supporter of the Anglo-Irish Treaty of 1921, which ended the Anglo-Irish war (1918-21) and established the Irish Free State (occ. pej.). O'Casey, *J*, 100: "Ah, why didn't I remember that then he wasn't a Diehard or a Stater, but only a poor dead son!" See: Diehard. [For ideological reasons, some extreme Republicans who opposed the Free State, such as those depicted in *An Giall* (1958), a play in Ir. by Brendan Behan, continued to use the term, even though the name of the state was changed to Eire (Ireland) in the new constitution adopted in 1937 and the state declared a republic in 1949.]

station(s)   *n.* the practice of celebrating Mass, with confessions and communion, in private houses in rural areas, usu. on a rotation basis, with the families involved providing food afterwards. Fitzmaurice, *R*, 85: "[T]isn't like the P.P. who can take what's put before him, he did for his three hard-boiled duck eggs indeed at my own station last week. . . ." See: P.P. ["Preparing for the Stations" is a chapter in Alice Taylor's memoir of an Irish country childhood, *To School Through The Fields* (1988); "doing the stations" is a com. phr. for the votive practice of the Stations of the Cross.]

stem see: stim.

sthrap see: strap.

sthravage (sthra, on the) see: stravage.

sthreel see: streel.

sthrippens see: strippings.

stick, up the see: up the pole.

stim (stem) *n.* an iota; usu. in references to sight. [H.E. var. of styme, Sc. and N. Engl. dial.] Corkery, *S*, 224: ". . . I won't have a stim of the sight left me soon."

stirk (sturk) *n.* a heifer or bullock about two years old; a pig about three months old; a thick-set person (pej.). [Engl. dial.] Friel, *P*, 76: ". . . I'd better catch up with the stirks before they do damage . . . ." Joyce, *FW*, 17.14: ". . . I can beuraly forstand a weird from sturk to finnic in such a patwhat as your rutterdamrotter." See: Bearla (beuraly).

stoir, a see: asthora.

stoned *a.* drunk (sl., Dub.). [Engl. sl.] Joyce, *FW*, 128.02: "[T]hough he's mildewstained he's mouldystoned . . . ." See: mouldy.

store (storeen, stooreen, storreen) see: asthora.

straak *n.* a share, a strip. [Var. of strake.] Fitzmaurice, *F*, 54: "[W]e having our own straak of drills to rise to. . . ."

straip see: strap.

stranger, the *met., euph.* the Norman and English invaders of Ireland (lit.). Joyce, *U*, 34: "A faithless wife first brought the strangers to our shore here, MacMurrough's wife and her leman O'Rourke, prince of Breffni." Cf. gall. [The details provided by Mr Deasy in this quot. from Joyce's *Ulysses* are inaccurate: the Normans invaded Ireland in 1169 at the invitation of Dermot MacMurrough, king of Leinster, who was exiled for eloping with, or abducting, Devorgilla, the wife of Tiernan O'Rourke, king of Breifne. "The Stranger" is a poem by Joseph Campbell.]

strap (sthrap, strapp, straip) *n.* a bold, forward or obnoxious female (pej.). [< Ir. *straip*, harlot.] Joyce, *U*, 771: "[Y]ou be damned you lying strap . . . ." Sayers, *P*, 71: "Hold the vessel right you thunderin' *straip* or I'll give you what I'm givin' the pig!" [The term appears in A.I. literature as early as the anon. ms. *Purgatorium Hibernicum* (ca. 1670-75).]

stravage (sthravage, stravaige, sthra) *v.* to roam about idly. Joyce, *U*, 303: "Mother kept a kip in Hardwicke street that used to be stravaging about the landings. . . at two in the morning without a stitch on her . . . ." See: kip.

streel (sthreel, streal)   *n., v.* a lazy, untidy woman (pej.); a slattern (occ. a male); to walk about untidily dressed. [< Ir. *sraoille*, an untidy, awkward person.] Joyce, *U*, 360: "Cissy came up along the strand . . . with her hat anyhow on her to one side after her run and she did look a streel . . . with the flimsy blouse she bought only a fortnight before like a rag on her back and a bit of her petticoat hanging like a carricature." O'Casey, *D*, 61: "That giddy, impudent sthreel who was here to tidy and polish th' room . . . ." Synge, *P*, 119: "An ugly young streeler with a murderous gob on him and a little switch in his hand." Corkery, *S*, 129: "[H]e went uselessly and restlessly strealing about his straggling fields . . . ." See: gob.

streeleen   *n.* a trail or stream of talk or gossip. [< Ir. *sraoill*, a trail, + een, H.E. dim. suf. < Ir. *ín*.] Synge, *P*, 81: "If you weren't destroyed travelling you'd have as much talk and streeleen, I'm thinking, as Owen Roe O'Sullivan or the poets of Dingle Bay [Co. Kerry] . . . ." [Owen Roe O'Sullivan (1748-1784), a Kerry poet who has been called a Gaelic Robert Burns, wrote some famous *aislingí*, such as *Ceo Draoidheachta (Magical Mist)*; see: aisling.]

strip   see: slip.

stroke-haul   *n., v.* a series of hooks or a grapnel used for fishing or recovering an object from a river. Corkery, *M*, 145: ". . . Jack Heffernan . . . handled the rope to to which the stroke-haul was fixed, while his son, Jim, grasping a long pole, stood ready to catch the body when it would have come near the surface." Somerville and Ross, *RM*, 83: ". . . I finished the notes I had been making on an adjourned case of stroke-hauling salmon in the Lonen River." [As the Somerville and Ross quot. suggests, the method is used for poaching, esp. salmon.]

strong farmer   *n.* a prosperous farmer with a large farm. Synge, *P*, 69: ". . . I the son of a strong farmer. . . , God rest his soul, could have bought up the whole of your old house a while since from the butt of his tail-pocket and not have missed the weight of it gone." [Some idea of what was considered a large farm can be gathered from *Tracy's Ambition* (1829), a novel by Gerald Griffin: a farmer with fifty acres is described as being "very strong".]

strool   *a.* muddled (pej.). [< Ir. *struille*, untidy, confused.] Joyce, *U*, 771: ". . . O wasnt I the born fool to believe all his blather about home rule and the land league sending me that long strool of a song out of the Huguenots to sing in French to be more classy . . . ."

sturk   see: stirk.

sugan (sugaun, sugawn, suggain, suggaun, suggawn, soogaun, sougawn)   *n.* a rope of hay or straw, a saddle or chair of such material; a collar of hay or straw placed around the neck of a student in a hedge school to indicate he is a dunce. [Ir. *súgán*.] Joyce, *P*, 236: "Lead him home with a sugan the way you'd lead a bleating goat." Corkery, *H*, 116: "Nicholas . . . swung her across the floor and planted her near the hearth on the remaining sugawn chair that was always there." See: hedge school. [This term appears in A.I. literature as early as the anon. ms. *Purgatorium Hibernicum* (ca. 1670-75); James Fitzthomas Fitzgerald, created Earl of Desmond by Red Hugh O'Neill in 1598, was dismissed as the Sugan (Straw or Bogus) Earl by the English; "Sugawn Chair" is a short story by Sean O'Faolain (1900-92).

summmach (summachaun)   *n.* a soft innocent child, or person. [< Ir. *somachán*.] Gregory, *P*, 91: ". . . Andy Hegarty, had a little chap — a little *summmach* of four years . . . ."

Swaddler (swadlere)   *n.* a Methodist, a Protestant (pej.). Joyce, *D*, 22: "[W]e walked on, the ragged troop screaming after us: *Swaddlers! Swaddlers!* thinking that we were Protestants. . . ." Cf. soupers, take soup, boiled Protestant. [There are Catholic and Protestant accounts of the origin of the term: a Catholic who converted to Protestantism for material rewards such as clothing; according to the main Protestant account, an ignorant Dublin priest, hearing one of the early Methodist preachers speak of "the babe in swaddling clothes," nicknamed the new sect Swaddlers. The latter account is close to that given by Charles Wesley (1707-1788) and recorded, with reservations, in the *OED*. The origin of the term was the subject of an exchange in *Notes and Queries*, March and April 1868; orig. applied to Methodists only, it was later, as in the quot. from Joyce's *Dubliners*, extended to all Protestants.]

swaddy (squaddy)   *n.* a British Army soldier (sl.). [Br. army sl.] Campbell, *P*, 256: "O, she's too rich for a Poddle swaddy, / With her tortoise comb and mantle fine."

Sweep, the   *n.* a lottery conducted by Irish Hospital Sweepstakes for the purpose of raising money for free medical treatment. Joyce, *FW*, 618.11: "We are advised the waxy is at the present in the Sweeps hospital and that he may never come out!" See: waxy. [The first Sweep was held in 1930, with a first prize of £208,792. Increasing competition from other and larger lotteries in recent years eventually forced its demise. *The Big Sweep* (1932) is a play by M. M. Brennan; *The Clean Sweep* (1968) by Arthur Webb is a history of the lottery.]

swither (swether)   *v.* to act indecisively (Uls.). [Sc.] Irvine, *L*, 120: "I begun t' swither whin she left."

taggeen   *n.* a glass of raw whiskey. Somerville and Ross, *RM*, 10: "[M]e A'nt said, would ye like a taggeen?" See: een.

Taig (Tague, Teague, Teig, Teige, Teigue, Theague, Thady)   *n.* a Roman Catholic (pej., Uls.); a plebeian Irishman. [< Ir. *Tadhg*, a poet; the name Thaddeus or Timothy, a typically plebeian Irish name.] O'Casey, *D*, 72: "[W]ho's Teig, what is dee decree, and who is dee debitee?" Joyce, *FW*, 176.13: ". . . *Heali Baboon and the Forky Theagues* . . . ." MacLaverty, *S*, 1: ". . . Roman Catholics. There's something spooky about them. Taigs." [The speaker in the O'Casey quot. is asking about a popular, 17th c., anti-Catholic song, "Lili Burlero"; the quot. from Joyce's *Finnegans Wake* is an attack on the politician Timothy Healy (1855-1931), enemy of Joyce's hero, Charles Stewart Parnell (1846-1891); Teague is the name of the Irish servant in *The Twin Rivals* (1702) by George Farquhar (1667-1707); Thady is the narrator of the first A.I. novel, *Castle Rackrent* (1800), by Maria Edgeworth; "Teige's Rambles" is a tune.]

take soup see: soup, take

take your hour see: hour, hold (take) your

Tanaiste see: tanist.

tanist (tannist) *n.* second-in-command; successor apparent to a king or chief, elected during his predecessor's lifetime. [< Ir. *tánaiste.*] Joyce, *U*, 43: "Lover, for her love he prowled with colonel Richard Burke, tanist of his sept, under the walls of Clerkenwell and, crouching, saw a flame of vengeance hurl them upward in the fog." [*A View of the Present State of Ireland* (ca. 1596), by Edmund Spenser, contains one of the earliest accounts in Engl. of the process by which a tanist is elected and assumes power on the death of chief. An Tanaiste is the title of the Deputy Taoiseach (Prime Minister) of Ireland.]

tanner *n.* a sixpence (sl.). [Engl. sl.] O'Casey, *P*, 148: "PETER: Heads, a juice. / FLUTHER: Harps, a tanner." See: head or harp, juice.

Tans see: Black and Tans.

Taoiseach see: tanist.

tare (tare and ages, tare-and-agers, tare and ouns, tare-an'-ounty, tare-an'-outy, taranagers, tatthar-an-agers, thunder and ounze, tundher and ouns, thunder and turf, blur an agers, blur and ages, blur an ouns, murder an' ages) *excl.* [< tears or blood and agues or wounds (of Christ).] Joyce, *U*, 412: "Tare and ages, what way would I be resting at all, he muttered thickly, and I tramping Dublin this while back with my share of songs and himself after me the like of a soulth or a bullawurrus?" Yeats, *M*, 50: "Tare-and-agers, girls, which av yez owns the child?" See: himself, soulth, bullawurrus. [The quot. from Joyce's *Ulysses* is one of a number of parodies in the work of the rendering of Irish folk speech by J. M. Synge and others; there is a pun on the excl. in Joyce's *Finnegans Wake*: "tearing ages" (582.02).]

tasby (taspy)   *n.* energy, spirit, sexual desire. [< Ir. *teaspach.*] Fitz-maurice, *F*, 72: "There do be great tasby in mermaids in the month of June." See: do be.

tasty   *a.* in good taste, respectable, elegant. Gregory, *SP*, 90: "It is so . . . you will be tasty coming in among the neighbours at Curranroe."

tatthar-an-agers   see: tare (and ages).

tay (tea)   *n.* tea, the evening meal. [18th c. Engl. pron. of tea, com. in H.E.] O'Casey, *J*, 76: "A bottle o' stout ud be a little too heavy for me stummock afther me tay . . . Ah-a-ah, I'll thry the ball o' malt." Joyce, *D*, 30: "[I]f Mangan's sister came out on the doorstep to call her brother in to his tea we watched her from our shadow peer up and down the street." See: ball of malt. [It was usu. in Ireland to have dinner in the middle of the day, and tea, a lighter cooked meal, in the evening.]

tay (tea), wet the   see: wet the tea.

tea   see: tea.

Teague   see: Taig.

Teernanogue   see: Tir na nOg.

Teig (Teige, Teigue)   see: Taig.

termon   *n.* land belonging to a religious house, a refuge, sanctuary or asylum (hist., lit.). [< Ir. *tearmann*, < L. *terminus.*] Campbell, *P*, 169: "I arise and face the east — / Golden termon / From which light, / Signed with dew and fire, / Dances."

The   *a.* denotes the chief of the clan bearing the surname which follows. Joyce, *FW*, 271.31-272.01: ". . . The O'Brien, The O'Connor, The Mac Loughlin and The Mac Namara . . . ." ["The O'Rahilly" is a poem by W. B. Yeats; in Joyce's *A Portrait of the Artist as a Young Man*, Stephen Dedalus is called "The Dedalus!" (168) by his classmates on Dollymount Strand.]

Theague   see: Taig.

them   *euph.* the fairies. Gregory, *P*, 91: "They thought it was the evil I had — that is given by *them* by a touch . . . ." Cf. away, gentle folk. [This euph. is a manifestation of a universal reluctance to name things that are feared.]

Thighearna, a   see: heirna.

thole   *v.* to endure, to bear (Uls.). [Sc.] Irvine, *L*, 135: " 'My God, Anna . . . ye wudn't be lavin' me alone . . . I can't thole it."

thon   *a.* yon, yonder, that (Uls.). [Comb. of the, or that, + yon.] Joyce, *U*, 426: "Wha gev ye thon colt?"

thonamon dux   see: manim an diouol.

thraneen (thrawneen, traneen, trawneen)   *n.* a piece of straw or dried grass; something worthless. [< Ir. *tráithnín.*] Synge, *P*, 113:

". . . I wouldn't give a thraneen for a lad hadn't a mighty spirit in him and a gamey heart." Yeats, *PO*, 296: "God be with the the times when I / Cared not a thrawneen for what chanced . . . ." O'Casey, *S*, 35: "Nobody now cares a traneen about the orders of the Ten Commandments . . . ."

thumping . . . craw   see: crawthumper.

thunder and ounze (turf)   see: tare (and ages).

Tierna, a   see: heirna.

till   *prep.* to (Uls.). [Sc.] Joyce, *FW*, 98.15: "Peacefully general astonishment assisted by regrettitude had put a term till his existence . . . ."

tilly   *n.* a small added measure given by milkmen, shopkeepers and the like to their customers; occ. used for a glass of whiskey. [< Ir. *tuilleadh*.] Joyce, *U*, 13: "She poured again a measureful and a tilly." Cf. duragh. ["Tilly" is the first of thirteen poems in Joyce's *Pomes Penyeach* (1927), but his purpose in placing the extra poem at the beginning of the collection rather than the end is not clear.]

tinned   *a.* wealthy (sl., Dub.). Joyce, *U*, 164: "The reverend Dr Salmon: tinned salmon. Well tinned in there."

tint   *n.* a small drink: usu. alcoholic spirits; a trace. [Engl. dial., a taste.] Fitzmaurice, *F*, 45: "[Y]ou must have a tint of something stronger than tea before you start. . . ." Corkery, *S*, 94: "She was called Litis because she was a cold sort of white, without a tint of warmth in it." See: litis.

Tir na nOg (Land of Youth, Tirnanoge, Teernanogue)   *n.* the Elysium of Irish mythology, a country of eternal happiness and pleasure in the western sea, where there is no sickness, age and death (lit.). [Ir. *Tír na nÓg*.] Joyce, *U*, 195: "East of the sun, west of the moon: *Tir na n-og*." Fitzmaurice, *F*, 9: "[I]t's the strange music that is entirely like what they do be playing in Teernanogue . . . ." A.E., *P*, 197: "[J]oyful winds are blowing from the Land of Youth to me . . . ." See: do be. [Tir na nOg is the setting of the bulk of "The Wanderings of Oisin" (1889), a narrative poem by W. B. Yeats; "In Tirnanoge" is a poem by A.E. (George Russell); *Thompson in Tir na nOg* (1918) is a play by Gerald MacNamara (1866-1938); *The Land of Youth* (1964) is a novel by Richard Power (1928-1970).]

Tom Trot's dog, like   see: Lanty McHale's dog.

tooth in it (them), not to put a (put no tooth, without putting a tooth)   *s. phr.* to speak openly or bluntly. Corkery, *H*, 68: "[W]ithout putting a tooth in them I flung a handful of terrible words up in their very mouths."

Top of the morning   *sal., c. phr.* Somerville and Ross, *B*, 192: "You've the top o' the morning and all the world before you." Shaw,

J, 409: "Man alive, don't you know that all this top-o-the-morning and broth-of-a-boy and more-power-to-your-elbow business is got up in England to fool you, like the Albert Hall concerts of Irish music. No Irishman ever talks like that in Ireland, or ever did, or ever will." See: more power. [As a sal. this phr. is considered an epitome of Irish speech outside of Ireland and of stage-Irish speech in Ireland; *Top of the Morning* (1920) is a collection of short stories by Seumas MacManus (1861-1960).]

tory   *n.* a fugitive, an outlaw; one of the dispossessed Irish of the 17th c. who survived by plundering the English planters. [< Ir. *tóir*, the act of hunting or pursuing.] Corkery, *H*, 11: "Their forefathers had been doing as much for the hunted Gaels of four centuries – those shadowy, unnamed warriors, poets, stragglers, kernes, galloglasses, tories, rapparees, outlaws, whiteboys, fenians . . . ." See: Gael, kerne, galloglass, rapparee, whiteboy, Fenian.

tosser   *n.* a coin, usu. a penny (sl.); from the use of coins in the game of pitch-and-toss. O'Casey, *P*, 148: "Which of yous has th' tossers."

Tostal (An)   *n.* a short-lived, spring cultural festival started in 1953; although it still survives (1991) in Drumshanbo, Co. Leitrim. [Ir. *tóstal*, an assembly, a pageant.] O'Casey, *D*, 38: "Hurrah for th' Tostal O, / That tempts us from our sleeping O, / When Erin sings and laughs and shouts, / Instead of always weeping O!" [There was a notable public controversy over *The Drums of Father Ned*, a play about preparations for the festival by Sean O'Casey, which was to receive its world premier during the 1958 Tostal. As a result, the play was not performed, and planned performances of *Bloomsday*, a dramatization of Joyce's *Ulysses* and *All That Fall* (1957), a radio play by Samuel Beckett, were cancelled. O'Casey's play was eventually produced in London in 1959.]

touch   *n.* sexual intercourse (sl.). [Br. sl.] Joyce, *U*, 89: "Give us a touch, Poldy. God, I'm dying for it."

touch of the relic   see: relic.

tram (tramp)   *n.* a small cock of hay. Gregory, *SP*, 37: "We'll get a share of it into tramps today."

traneen (trawneen)   see: thraneen.

treenahayla   *a.* mixed up in confusion. [< Ir. *trí na chéile*, through each other.] Fitzmaurice, *F*, 36: "They are treenahayla and striking wild."

trot a mouse (horse) on it, You could   *s. phr.* applied to tea which is particularly strong. Joyce, *FW*, 456.01: "That was a damn good cup of scald! You could trot a mouse on it."

Troubles, the   *n.* the period of revolution in Ireland which began in 1916 and led to the establishment of the Irish Free State in

1922, followed by a brief civil war, 1922-23; now applied to the cur. conflict in Northern Ireland which erupted about 1969; occ. used for periods of unrest before 1916. Joyce, *D*, 31: "[S]treet singers . . . sang a *come-all-you* about O'Donovan Rossa or a ballad about the troubles in our native land." See: come-all-you. [Jeremiah O'Donovan Rossa (1831-1915) in the quot. from Joyce's *Dubliners* was a Fenian leader; his burial at Glasnevin Cemetery in Dublin, on August 1, 1915, was the occasion of a famous oration by Patrick Pearse, leader of the 1916 Rising; see: Fenian.]

tuata *n.* a rustic, an unskilled labourer (lit.). [Ir. *tuata*.] Campbell, *P*, 217: "Who of this motley crowd / Is . . . A tuata?"

tundher and ouns see: tare (and ages).

turbary *n.* bogland on which there is an ancient right to cut turf (peat). [M.E. < A.F. *turberie*.] Synge, *P*, 117: "Would you give me . . . turbary upon the western hill." [Turbary-right was dependent on land holding, but the land to which the right attached did not necessarily adjoin the bog.]

turnover *n.* a loaf of bread shaped somewhat like a boot. Joyce, *FW*, 12.16: "So true is it that therewhere's a turnover the tay is wet too . . . ." See: wet the tea (the tay is wet).

Turra mon dhiol see: dhiol.

uaisht see: whisht.

Ugh see: Och.

ul-ullalu see: alilu.

Uladh (Ulla) *n.* Ulster. [< Ir. *Ulaidh*.] Yeats, *PL*, 171: "Conchubar . . ., the old king of Uladh . . . is still strong and vigorous. . . ." A.E., *P*, 231: "The Hound of Ulla lies, with those who shed / Tears for the Wild Geese fled." See: wild geese. [The Hound of Ulla (occ. Culann) is Cuchulain (< Ir. *cú*, hound), hero of the Red Branch cycle of mythological tales.]

ullagone (hullagone, oolaghaun, ulican) *v., n.* to lament; the traditional refrain of the keen. [< Ir. *olagón*.] Fitzmaurice, *F*, 17: "MAINEEN *and* AUNT JUG *commence to ullagone; they keen louder and louder as tumultuous voices are heard approaching*". Corkery, *S*, 149: "He stopped up his rambling hulagoning . . . ." See: een, keen.

ullalu see: alilu.

uncle *n.* a pawnbroker (sl., euph.). O'Casey, *J*, 89: ". . . I suppose you remember me lendin' you some time ago three pouns that I raised on blankets an' furniture in me uncle's?" [Three brass balls are the traditional sign of pawnbrokers.]

Uncrowned King [**of Ireland**] *c. phr.* Charles Stewart Parnell (1846-1891), leader of the Irish Party and Home Rule Movement in the British House of Commons (1879-90). Joyce, *D*, 134: "*Our*

Uncrowned King is dead." [The phr. was first applied to Parnell by Timothy Healy (1855-1931) at a fund-raising meeting in Canada in March, 1880; Healy is the subject of Joyce's "Et Tu, Healy"; Parnell is a highly symbolic figure in the works of Yeats and Joyce.]

Union *n.* a workhouse for the destitute. [Engl.] Synge, *P*, 2, 143: "Then I'd best be going to the Union beyond, and there'll be a welcome before me, I tell you . . . ."

up from the bog (up on the last load)   see: bog, up from the

up on my back, climbing   see: back, in my

up the pole (stick)   *s. phr.* in a predicament: usu. applied to unmarried women who are pregnant (sl.). O'Casey, *P*, 108: "I'm up the pole; no more dhrink for Fluther."

'Usha   see: musha.

usquebagh (usquebaugh, uishge)   *n.* whiskey. [< Ir. *uisce beatha*, water of life (whiskey).] Fitzmaurice, *F*, 108: "Here's usquebagh woman. . . ." Joyce, *U*, 199: "Three drams of usquebaugh you drank with Dan Deasy's ducats."

vic, a (vich, a)   see: avic.

vo   *interj.* alas, woe. [Perh. < Ir. *boch*.] Corkery, *S*, 53: "Every now and then the grey old head of the drooping figure in it would move from side to side, and 'Vo! Vo! Vo! Vo!' — the traditional Irish cry of sorrow — would break from the lips."

voteen   *n.* a very devout person (occ. pej.). [Perh. < devotee, or < Ir. *módín*, a devotee.] Yeats, *M*, 280: "I saw that he was also a voteen, as the peasants say, for there was a rosary hanging from a nail on the rim of the barrel. . . ." See: een.

vourneen   see: mavourneen.

wain (wean)   *n.* a child (Uls.). [Sc.] Irvine, *L*, 93: "Maybe Mrs Boyle an' the wains are as hungry as we are. . . ."

wake   *a.* weak. [18th c. Engl. pron. of weak, com. in H.E.] Joyce, *FW*, 496.15: "[O]ld Eire wake as Piers Aurell was flappergangsted." See: Eire. [Prominent as a pun in the title and throughout Joyce's *Finnegans Wake*.]

wall, dry   see: dry wall.

wan   see: one.

warrant, a (good, great, bad)   *n., s. phr.* in possession of, or lacking, a particular skill. Synge, *P*, 85: "[I]f she found you were such a warrant to talk, she'd be stringing gabble till the dawn of day." *Ibid.*, 59. ". . . Marcus Quinn, God rest him, got six months for maming ewes, and he a great warrant to tell stories of holy Ireland. . . ." [Good warrant appears in A.I. literature as early as Jonathan Swift's *A Dialogue in Hibernian Style* (1735).]

waxie (waxies') Dargle *n.* annual picnic (iron.); from the annual picnic of Dublin's waxies (cobblers): the gentry went to such fashionable places as the Dargle Valley in Co. Wicklow; the waxies went to closer and more plebeian places, such as Ringsend, Irishtown and Sandymount Strand. Joyce, *U*, 147: "Out for the waxies' Dargle. Two old trickies, what?" See: waxy. ["The Waxies' Dargle" is a song; "We fell into the Waxies' Dargle" is a section of *Hold your hour and have another* (1963), by Brendan Behan. There is now a stone in Pembroke Street, Irishtown, marking the approximate location of this annual event.]

waxy *n.* a cobbler (nic.); from their use of wax. Joyce, *FW*, 618.11: "We are advised the waxy is at the present in the Sweeps hospital and that he may never come out!" See: sweep; cf. waxie Dargle.

wean see: wain.

wee folk (people) see: gentle folk.

weekly insult *c. phr.* wages (iron., Cork). Joyce, *FW*, 42.03: "[He was] . . . a decent sort of the hadbeen variety who had just been touching the weekly insult . . . ."

weerasthrue see: wirrasthrue.

weir asthrue (weirastru) see: wirrasthrue.

weira see: wirra.

west (wesht) *adv.* back. [< Ir. *siar*, west, back (implying motion).] Somerville and Ross, *RME*, 199: "Move west a small piece, Mary Jack, if you please . . . ." Cf. east. [Traditionally in Ireland the cardinal points were designated on the assumption that one faced east; hence, *soir* (eastward, forward) and *siar* (westward, backward); according to an apocryphal story, an Irish boy excused himself for not washing behind his ears by saying, " 'twas too far wesht!" The delusive meanderings of most Irish roads would make it impossible to travel for any significant distance by compass direction.]

West Briton (Brit) *c. phr.* a pro-British Irishman (pej.); orig. a Protestant loyalist: one of a number of pej. terms for those who supported, or were suspected of supporting, Br. rule in Ireland. Joyce, *D*, 190: "[S]he had no right to call him a West Briton before people, even in a joke." Cf. Castle Catholic, Castle hack, shoneen. [In "The Dead", a story in Joyce's *Dubliners*, Gabriel Conroy is accused of being a West Briton on the slender evidence of writing book reviews for a pro-Br. newspaper, *The Daily Express*. The phr. is used occ. in Uls. for a Dubliner.]

wet, a *n.* an alcoholic drink (sl.). O'Casey, *J*, 66: "An' now, Mr. Bentham, you'll have to have a wet."

wet and dry *s. phr.* constant, usu. used to describe employment of a kind that is not interrupted by the notoriously fickle Irish weather. Joyce, *CW*, 243: "'Twas Irish humour, wet and dry, / Flung quicklime into Parnell's eye . . . ." ["Irish Humour, Wet and Dry", is a section of *Rich and Rare: A Book of Ireland* (1987), comp. Sean McMahon.]

wet the tea (tay) *s. phr.* to make tea; a euph. for sexual intercourse. Sayers, *P*, 60: "To see a grain of tea at that time was a great rarity but Maire brought some back from Dingle and then she wet the tea." Joyce, *FW*, 585.31: "You never wet the tea!" [The context of the quot. from Joyce's *Finnegans Wake* clearly indicates its sexual connotations; the phr. is the basis of a pun on the name of the Scottish river Tay earlier in the work: "the tay is wet" (12.16).]

wheen *n.* a small number or quantity (Uls.). [Sc.] Irvine, *L*, 53: "Oh, jist a few sheep's throtters and a wheen of nettles."

whisht (whishth, whist, husth, uaisht; hold your whisht / whist / wheesht / whuisht) *excl.* be quiet, hold your tongue, listen. [< Ir. *(bí id') thost*.] O'Casey, *S*, 26: "Whisht! What's that?" Corkery, *S*, 111: "[W]hen I'm speaking, let ye hold yer whishth!"

whisteroo see: wirrasthrue.

white martyrdom see: martyrdom, red (white)

Whiteboy *n.* a member of a secret society founded in Tipperary in 1761, for the purpose of committing what the authorities called "agrarian outrages" against the excesses of landlords; from the white shirts they wore at night to better identify each other. Corkery, *H*, 11: "Their forefathers had been doing as much for the hunted Gaels of four centuries — those shadowy, unnamed warriors, poets, stragglers, kernes, galloglasses, tories, rapparees, outlaws, whiteboys, fenians . . . ." See: Gael, kerne, galloglass, tory, rapparee, Fenian.

whuisht see: whisht.

wierasthru see: wirrasthrue.

wigs on the [village] green *c. phr.* a fight, a commotion. Joyce, *U*, 352, "[I]f he took it there'd be wigs on the green . . . ." [The phr. may have its origin in faction fighting, which was com. at fairs and other public gatherings in Ireland from the 17th to the mid 19th c.; see: back.]

wild geese, the *met.* Jacobite Irish soldiers who fled to Europe after, and in accordance with, the conditions of the Treaty of Limerick, 1691; Irish exiles. Campbell, *P*, 187: "*When the wild geese cry, the west listens. / I died not for my own, / But my own love me.*" Cf. blackbird. [The speaker in the Joseph Campbell quot. is the most famous of the wild geese, Patrick Sarsfield, who went to France with about 12,000 troops, joined the Irish Brigade, was mortally wounded in the battle of Landen and died on July 23, 1693. On seeing the blood from his wounds, he is reputed to have said: "Oh, that this were for Ireland!" The artist is consistently linked with the wild geese in Joyce's *A Portrait of the Artist as a Young Man*, *Ulysses* and *Finnegans Wake*. "The Wild Geese" is a poem by William Drennan (1745-1820) and a novel (1938) by Bridget Boland; *With the Wild Geese* (1902) is a volume of poems by Emily Lawless (1845-1913); "The Wild Goose" (1903) is a story in *The Untilled Field* by George Moore, and a play (1936) by Teresa Deevy (1903-1963); *The Wild Geese: The Irish Soldier in Exile* (1973) is a book by Maurice Hennessy (1906-).]

wind, raise the   see: raise the wind.

wing   *n.* a penny (sl., Dub.): obs. since decimalization of currency in 1971. [Var. of win (Engl. sl.), a penny.] Joyce, *U*, 426: "Two bar and a wing." See: bar. [The pre-decimal Irish penny (1928-1971) depicted a hen with her wing extended protectively over her clutch of chickens, but the term was in use in Ireland earlier than 1928, as the quot. from Joyce's *Ulysses* (1922) indicates.]

wink is a good as a nod to a blind horse, a   see: nod is as good as a wink to a blind horse, a

wipe   *n.* a blow. [Engl. sl.] Joyce, *P*, 182: "One of the Crokes made a woeful wipe at him one time with his camann . . . ." See: caman (camann).

wiristhru   see: wirrasthru.

wirra (weira, mwirra, worra, wurra, wurrah, a-wurrah, amirra)   *excl.* indicates sorrow, surprise or vexation. [< Ir. *A Mhuire*, O (Virgin) Mary.] Fitzmaurice, *F*, 108: "Oh, wirra, wirra, the Big Eel having him again." Fitzmaurice, *R*, 10: "Amirra, I'm thinking Michaeleen Quirke gave more blood after the first miss than this man after three. . . ." See: een; cf. wirrasthrue.

wirrasthrue (wirrastroo, wirrastrua, wiristhru, wierasthru, weir asthru, weirasthru, weerasthrue, wurristroo, wurra strew, wurrustrew, whisteroo)   *excl., a.* indicating sorrow, surprise or vexation; pitiful. [< Ir. *A Mhuire is truagh*, O (Virgin) Mary it is a pity.] Joyce, *SH*, 113: "Doesn't he look like a wirrasthrue Jaysus? said Stephen pointing to the Tsar's photograph and using the Dublin version of the name as an effective common noun." See: Jaysus; cf. wirra.

wish 1   see: great wish.

wish 2   *n.* vulva, vagina (sl., Dub.). Joyce, *FW*, 202.34: "She thought she's sankh neathe the ground with nymphant shame when he gave her the tigris eye! O happy fault! Me wish it was he!"

wisha   see: Musha.

within an ass's bawl   see: ass's bawl.

without putting a tooth in it (them)   see: tooth in it (them).

woman of the house   *s.phr.* the mistress, housewife. [< Ir. *bean an tighe.*] Joyce, *U*, 499: "Let me be going now woman of the house, for by all the goats in Connemara I'm after having the father and mother of a bating." See: father and mother; cf. banatee, man of the house. [The quot. from Joyce's *Ulysses* is one of a number of a parodies in the work of the rendering of Irish folk speech by J. M. Synge and others; "The Woman of the House" is a poem by Richard Murphy (1927-).]

worra   see: wirra.

wurra (wurrah)   see: wirra.

wurra strew   see: wirrasthrue.

Yarra (Yerra)   see: Arrah.

Yellow John (George)   see: Shane Bwee.

Yirrah   see: Arrah.

yoke   *n.* a contraption, a vehicle, anything complicated: the H.E. equivalent of "thingamajig." Joyce, *P*, 182: "[I] missed the train home and I couldn't get any kind of yoke to give me a lift . . . ."

You could sing that if you had an air to it   *c. phr.* a response to a remark that is obviously true. O'Casey, *J*, 61: "You could sing that if you had an air to it!"

Youth, Land of   see: Tir na nOg.

BIBLIOGRAPHY

Aldus, Judith Butler. "Anglo-Irish Dialects: a Bibliography, Enlarged Version." *Regional Language Studies*. Newfoundland: [Memorial University], no. 7, 22 June, 1976.

Baumgarten, Rolf. *Bibliography of Irish Linguistics and Literature, 1942-71*. Dublin: Institute for Advanced Studies, 1986.

Bliss, Alan. *Spoken English in Ireland 1600-1740*. Dublin: The Dolmen Press; New Jersey: Humanities Press, 1979.

A Book of Irish Quotations. Ed. Sean McMahon. Dublin: The O'Brien Press, 1984.

Boylan, Henry. *A Dictionary of Irish Biography*. Dublin: Gill and Macmillan, 1978.

Brady, Anne and Brian Cleeve. *A Biographical Dictionary of Irish Writers*. Gigginstown, Co. Westmeath: The Lilliput Press, 1985.

Braidwood, John. *The Ulster Dialect Lexicon*. Belfast: The Queen's University, 1969.

Clark, James M. *The Vocabulary of Anglo-Irish*. St. Gallen: Zollikofer, 1917.

The Compact Edition of the Oxford English Dictionary. 2 vols. Oxford: Oxford University Press, 1979.

The Concise Scots Dictionary. Ed. Mairi Robinson. Aberdeen: Aberdeen University Press, 1985.

Corkery, Daniel. *The Hidden Ireland*. Dublin: M. H. Gill and Son, 1967.

The Course of Irish History. Ed. T. W. Moody and F. X. Martin. Cork: The Mercier Press, 1984.

Croghan, Martin J. *Demythologizing Hiberno-English*. Boston: Northeastern University (Working Papers in Irish Studies, 90-1), 1990.

Curtis, Edmund. *A History of Ireland*. London: Methuen and Co., 1968.

Danaher, Kevin. *The Year in Ireland*. Cork: Mercier Press, 1972.

Deane, Seamus. *A Short History of Irish Literature*. London: Hutchinson & Co.; Indiana: University of Notre Dame Press, 1986.

A Dictionary of Catch Phrases. Ed. Eric Partridge. London: Routledge and Keegan Paul, 1977.

A Dictionary of Cork Slang. Comp. Seán Beecher. Cork: Goldy Angel Press, 1983.

A Dictionary of Irish History 1800-1980. Comp. D. J. Hickey and J. E. Doherty. Dublin: Gill and Macmillan, 1987.

Dictionary of Irish Literature. Ed. Robert Hogan. Dublin: Gill and Macmillan, 1985.

A Dictionary of Irish Mythology. Comp. Peter Berresford Ellis. Oxford: Oxford University Press, 1990.

1811 Dictionary of the Vulgar Tongue. Comp. Francis Grose. London: Bibliophile Books, 1984.

Dictionary of Newfoundland English. Eds. G. M. Story, W. J. Kirwin and J. P. A. Widdowson. Toronto: University of Toronto Press, 1982.

A Dictionary of Slang and Unconventional English. 2 vols. Ed. Eric Partridge. London: Routledge and Keegan Paul, 1980.

Dillon, Myles. *Early Irish Literature.* Chicago: The University of Chicago Press, 1965.

The English Dialect Dictionary. 6 vols. Ed. Joseph Wright. London: Henry Frowde, 1889-1905.

English-Irish Dictionary. Ed. Tomás de Bhaldraithe. Baile Átha Cliath: Oifig an tSoláthair, 1959.

The English Language in Ireland. Ed. Diarmaid O Muirithe. Dublin: The Mercier Press, 1977.

Evans, E. Estyn. *Irish Folk Ways.* London: Routledge and Kegan Paul, 1957.

Foclóir Gaedhilge agus Béarla: An Irish-English Dictionary. Comp. and ed. Patrick S. Dinneen. Dublin: The Educational Book Company of Ireland, 1927.

Foclór Gaeilge-Béarla. Eag. Niall O Donaill. Baile Átha Cliath: Oifig an tSoláthair, 1977.

Foster, R. F. *Modern Ireland 1660-1972.* London: Penguin Books, 1989.

Irish University Review. Special issue: "The English of the Irish." Ed. T. P. Dolan. vol. 20, no. 1 (Spring 1990).

Jeffares, A. Norman. *Anglo-Irish Literature.* Dublin: Gill and Macmillan, 1982.

Joyce, P. W. *English as we speak it in Ireland.* London: Longmans, Green, & Co.; Dublin: M. H. Gill and Son, 1910.

——. *Old Irish Folk-Music and Songs.* New York: Cooper Square Publishers, 1965.

Kiberd, Declan. *Synge and the Irish Language.* London: The Macmillan Press, 1979.

The Living Webster Encyclopedic Dictionary of the English Language. Chicago: The English Language Institute of America, 1977.

Lyons, F. S. L. *Ireland Since the Famine.* London, Fontana Press, 1987.

McHugh, Roger and Maurice Harmon. *Short History of Anglo-Irish Literature.* Dublin: Wolfhound Press, 1982.

Papers on Irish English. Ed. Dónaill P. O Baoill. Dublin: Irish Association for Applied Linguistics, 1985.

Perspectives on the English Language in Ireland. Ed. John Harris et. al. Dublin: Centre for Language and Communications Studies, Trinity College, 1986.

Power, Patrick C. *The Story of Anglo-Irish Poetry (1800-1922).* Cork: The Mercier Press, 1967.

Proverbs & Sayings of Ireland. Ed. Sean Gaffney and Seamus Cashman. Dublin: The Wolfhound Press, 1974.

Royal Irish Academy Committee for the Study of Anglo-Irish Language and Literature. *Handlist of work in progress and work completed in Anglo-Irish dialect studies.* Dublin, November 1972.

——. Miscellaneous Unpublished Anglo-Irish Dialect Word Lists.

The Scottish National Dictionary. 10 vols. Edinburgh: The Scottish National Dictionary Association, vol. 1, n. d., vol. 10, 1976.

The Shorter Oxford English Dictionary. 2 vols. Oxford: Clarendon Press, 1977.

Smyth, Daragh. *A Guide to Irish Mythology.* Dublin: Irish Academic Press, 1988.

Todd, Loreto. *Words Apart: A Dictionary of Northern Ireland English.* Gerrards Cross: Colin Smythe, 1990.

Ulster Dialects: An Introductory Symposium. Ed. G. B. Adams. Holywood, Co. Down: Ulster Folk Museum, 1964.

Ulster-English Dictionary. Comp. John Pepper. Belfast: Appletree Press, 1981.

Van Hamlel, A. G. *On Anglo-Irish Syntax.* Chicago: The University of Chicago, 1977.

Wall, Richard. *An Anglo-Irish Dialect Glossary for Joyce's Works.* Gerrards Cross: Colin Smythe, 1986; New York: Syracuse University Press, 1987.